23.3.72

THE CHARACTER OF TOWNS

Roy Worskett ARIBA AMTPI

THE CHARACTER OF TOWNS

An Approach to Conservation

The Architectural Press, London

85139 121 4

First published 1969

Second impression 1970

© Architectural Press 1969

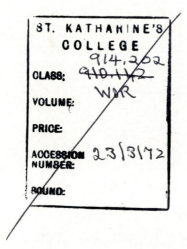
Made and printed in Great Britain by
William Clowes and Sons, Limited
London and Beccles

CONTENTS

FOREWORD

Much of the material and experience which go to the making of this book are derived from my work in the Ministry of Housing and Local Government. I am grateful to the Ministry for facilitating the preparation of this book and for giving me permission to publish. I should emphasise that the views expressed in it are my own and do not commit the Ministry in any way.

It is often suggested that it is possible to judge the quality of an age or society by the way in which it cares for its elderly people. It is also increasingly true to say that one can judge a society by the degree to which it allows the qualities of its urban or rural environment to be destroyed, either inadvertently or by purposeful vandalism. The archaeological, architectural and visual qualities of our many historic towns can make a considerable contribution to the quality of our environment if we realise their value and urgently take action to conserve them. This involves everyone—not only the architects and town planners but everyone with eyes to use and the will to make a fuss.

Following the passing of the Civic Amenities Act in 1967 more attention is being given to the conservation of the character and identity of towns. It is essential that the Act should be interpreted broadly—conservation must mean more than simply preserving historic buildings—and this book sets out to show the wide range of interrelated townscape qualities that ought to be taken into account in drawing up a conservation policy. Furthermore it is suggested that these wider qualities can be a major factor in determining specific visual disciplines and codes for various aspects of the design of the new development in our existing towns.

Above all conservation must be seen within the framework of general planning policies. The main thesis of the book is based on the assumption that conservation need not be too heavy a financial burden providing its inherent limitations are accepted, and incorporated into planning policies. Whether the area concerned is a whole village, a small town, or part of a city centre, the conservation of its fabric will affect the degree of economic activity and growth, the accommodation of traffic and the amount and type of new development. It will inevitably determine certain social changes. Planning can only go so far to achieve all that is required. Vigilance and informed opinion will also be needed from both individuals and civic societies.

7

A word of warning—this book is not about the detailed problems of maintenance and restoration of historic buildings. No book can be a complete guide to all the facets of the character of every town, and in any case each town requires an individual approach. It seeks only to suggest a method of approach to conserving the character and identity of towns; to provide a check list of some of the things to look for in your town and of the policies that will help to maintain its character.

INTRODUCTION

Preservation is an idea surrounded with emotion. There are many people passionately for it, and just as many against it. If, however, you feel that there is value in being able to see and live with a town's past, you will no doubt be sympathetic to the aims of this book from the start. If, on the other hand, you believe that the more quickly we can erase the past and begin again the better, you are likely to be at odds with the book's underlying theme—conservation. You may, if you read on, eventually be convinced that conservation is not simply a matter of preservation, but can also be instrumental in creating new townscape.

The desire to preserve things is not new, but now change in our towns comes with such speed and on such a scale that most of us are affected by it in some way. It turns some people into rabid preservationists and it encourages others to think more closely about the nature of towns as we know them today and their future.

It may be quite reasonably argued that the generations who have lived through two world wars and on the edge of a final nuclear catastrophe for so long are more inclined to preservation than their predecessors—anything which expresses stability becomes important. If there is a psychological need for preservation it is part of the planner's job to take account of it.

Change is no enemy if we learn how to handle it. Physical change (that is change in the environment provided by our towns) reflects social change—change in our numbers, in our welfare and in our demands.

Until the end of the eighteenth century the pattern of life in this country was slow to change. The form and layout of towns and their architecture responded to the slowness of social development. The appearance of towns remained reasonably whole and complete. Visual design as an independent specialist skill was seldom a separate process. The materials and methods of building, together with the natural topography, created an evolving vernacular style or discipline.

In the nineteenth century a sudden leap into industrial activity drew people from the countryside into the fast expanding industrial towns. The railways carved the first system of mass transport through town and country; coal, iron and steel, the materials of the Industrial Revolution, became the keystones of social progress with correspondingly dramatic new developments in the layout and form of towns. Architecture often became the cushion to soften the blow; the great engineering works—the railway stations, the warehouses and the bridges—were faced in every conceivable style of architecture. The visual problems were partly overcome, sometimes mistakenly but often prettily, by masking them from view.

Throughout this great surge of change, and despite the coming of the railways, the scale and atmosphere of the historic core of the market towns remained visually intact and relatively undisturbed, socially. Some even survived as a nucleus for industrial expansion.

If some of these towns remained largely untouched almost to the present day it was due to the slowness with which industrial wealth percolated through society. In 1922 the first baby car rolled off the production line and initiated a new era; standardisation, personal mobility and consumer choice were on the way in; the fruits of industrialisation were about to be spread through wider sections of the community. This process has quickened and if forecasts are correct it is by no means finished. The ownership of cars, for example, is still a long way from its peak, and so, we are told, is our leisure time. Architecture can no longer mask the effects of change; indeed the best architecture has made them an ally, no longer seeking to disguise them, but using them for visual inspiration.

The last half of the twentieth century is rapidly bringing the old market towns and cathedral cities face to face with the symbols of a wealthier society. Cars and lorries are choking the medieval streets, beginning to tear open their compactness in order to move more quickly (if by now the vehicles can move at all). Offices and supermarkets are altering the domestic scale. The pressures cannot be ignored. Changing society creates the need for a changing environment.

That we must integrate these changes into the fabric of towns is unquestionable—financially we cannot afford (in all but a few new towns) to start again from scratch. How and where we achieve this integration without destroying the best of the existing fabric of our towns is the central theme of this book.

A glance at most old towns (and it is principally those free-standing towns and cities with which this book is concerned) will confirm, if confirmation is needed, that there is a problem, certainly it will also show that in some cases we are already too late with the solution. The conservation of the character of our existing towns is therefore an urgent matter. Unless we learn to resolve the conflict between preservation and change, to integrate the twentieth century sympathetically with its predecessors, our architectural heritage will be lost. More important still, the qualities of visual completeness and individuality that typify many of our older towns will be broken up and eroded away.

This book is therefore about our existing towns, their intrinsic visual qualities, and the differences between them; not just the so-called historic towns but all those with an individual identity. It describes some of the ways and means of maintaining these differences and suggests that the qualities we inherited from the past can become a discipline for change today. Its main thesis is that a town's past, its present and its future must combine to

10

The basic threat to our existing towns is that we no longer find them suitable or convenient for our use. They are old and in many cases beyond repair. Old buildings may be too small or too large and the demand for their use is often turned away because their environment is no longer suitable.

11

create a recognisable unit, so that its growth can be seen and felt to be continuous.

Society needs both cultural and physical roots and a town's visual and historic qualities can satisfy at least part of this need. That is why for so many people old-established towns seem so pleasant to live in. There is plenty of room for research here; we know very little about our conscious or subconscious reactions to the quality of our visual surroundings: on the little evidence available* there would seem to be some relationship between visual quality and social behaviour.

Quite apart from any sociological reasons there is a clear responsibility on both the professional and the layman, the councillor or the Civic Society member, to ensure that buildings of architectural or historic importance are effectively preserved as representative examples of their time. Their preservation is of course assisted, though not necessarily secured, by Act of Parliament.

But if change is inevitable and a degree of preservation desirable how do we resolve the conflict? How do we preserve our heritage effectively? How

* A relationship between pleasant visual surroundings and neighbourliness has been found in comparing different housing estates (Peter Wilmot and Richard MacCormac, *Architects' Journal*, 25th March, 1964).

Below: the biggest single cause of deterioration in the environment is traffic. Cars must move and be parked.

Shops must be serviced, yet in many places there is only just enough room for the pedestrian.

Above: the domestic scale of towns is challenged by new activities and the new scale of buildings to contain them. Below: we could often be more careful where we place these new large scale buildings so that the townscape retains some order, and individual buildings some significance. Here the new overpowers the old and devalues it. There is no longer a simple, understandable image.

Above: good architecture is perhaps, like beauty, in the eye of the beholder, but the way the architect emphasises the scale of this building would make it unacceptable within the domestic scale of most of our small towns.

Facing page, bottom:
there is also a need
for a sense of place:
it would not be sur-
prising to find these
new houses in the
countryside or be-
hind a small town.
You would certainly
not expect to find
them in hard, urban
Barnsbury in Lon-
don.

This page: bad
architecture is not al-
ways to blame for
the deterioration of
the environment. It
is often straight-
forward, unthinking,
untidy mess.

A different kind of mess, but just as destructive, is the undisciplined sprawl of buildings around the edges of our towns, taking no account of their existing form or the surrounding landscape.

do we maintain visual completeness between old and new? How do we maintain the character of towns? As I have already suggested, it is hoped to show that a conservation policy is not simply a matter of dealing with historic buildings, or areas which contain historic buildings, but is also a part of a creative process that can provide inspiration and discipline for change.

In practice, change is to some extent essential for preservation. Few buildings can reasonably be preserved as museum pieces. Conservation itself needs change. For example, many buildings have been preserved by implementing change—a Georgian mansion converted for use as a school or divided into flats is now commonplace. Bathrooms, hot water and drainage have all been incorporated to ensure effective preservation; and yet with a good architect the building retains its overall architectural identity. Here is a lesson for our towns. By seeing a town as a whole and considering preservation alongside the needs for change, we may enable our towns to retain their historic qualities and their individual identities without unnecessarily inhibiting a reasonable degree of essential growth and modernisation.

We must understand physical change and its basic social and economic origins. We must be clear about what we want to conserve, and why, and as part of the process of town planning we must develop techniques to cope with such a fundamental conflict. But success in this field not only depends on the adequacy of techniques but also on the vision and sensitivity of the architect-planner and on his ability to explain himself. The approach which is outlined throughout the following chapters is essentially about the job of the architect working with the planning team—the scope of the architect's work, what he must look for, and the policies he particularly must help to create. In some towns where historic or visual quality is of great importance he must be the leader of the team. He must, with the advice of archaeologist, historian and landscape architect, provide a survey and appraisal of the visual and historic qualities of the town as it stands, the contribution its history has made to its present appearance, and he must suggest how these might influence its future. He must however be aware that appearance is only one aspect of town planning; there are many other factors to be considered.

Buildings to be preserved

There are many buildings which are recognised as architecturally and historically important. Some are important locally, some nationally. Left: house in the Causeway, Horsham. Below: Bess Surtees' house, Newcastle.

I. APPROACH TO CONSERVATION

This chapter sets out to define what it is that we ought to conserve. We must also decide what is wrong, if anything, with the way in which change takes place now and which aspects of change we must discipline more strictly.

First, what are we trying to conserve? We have said that it is the character of a town. What makes up that character? What is it that makes one town different from the next, that makes the resident feel he is at home and gives the visitor a new experience in each town?

Historic buildings which are valuable for their architectural quality as acknowledged masterpieces of their time are an obvious starting-point. But there are other buildings which ought to be considered, buildings which illustrate a town's history through their association with people or events, local activities or styles and periods of architecture.

But these are by no means the only contributions to a town's identity. There is an experience to be gained from a visit to Liverpool which is quite distinct from that gained when visiting Manchester, when visiting Durham or Newcastle, Salisbury or Winchester. These differences are concerned with something more than discovering historic buildings. The social functions of a town, the influence of its geographical and political background, the local topography, will all have determined its siting and form in the same way that these influences, though different in content, determine the siting of new towns today. All these factors combine together to influence the appearance of the urban fabric or townscape.

In his book *Townscape* Gordon Cullen says: "One building standing alone in the countryside is experienced as architecture, but bring half a dozen buildings together and an art other than architecture is made possible". This is the art of townscape.

The importance of townscape is probably best illustrated by considering its effect on an individual building. We can usually grasp the qualities of a single building, but have had little experience in assessing those of a town as a whole. The sketches, pages 28–31, show how townscape affects the visual importance and value of a single building and how its intrinsic quality is apparently changed as its townscape setting changes.

We can therefore say that whilst individual buildings contribute to the overall quality and character of a town, they cannot be considered the only constituent part of that character, nor necessarily the most important part. Visually most towns derive their identity and personality from the way in which individual buildings, both good and not so good, together create a general atmosphere and build up a recognisable local townscape—a distinct Turn to page 31

19

Some buildings of all ages right up to the present day are worthy of retention, to illustrate the historic continuity of the town. Above: the Victorian Guildhall, Northampton (a listed building).

A house in Dorking, Surrey, that was surely worth keeping but has been demolished (an unlisted building).

An industrial building in Newcastle.

We could even grow to like this example from the inter-war years.

A building may be worth preserving if it was designed by a distinguished architect or was occupied by a famous man. Left: the designer of this one, in Hunter's Road, Birmingham, was Pugin. Below: the Jolly Farmer, Farnham, Surrey, was William Cobbett's home.

A building in Buchanan Street, Glasgow, which
could be retained for its unrepeatable ornamental
qualities.

22

There may be buildings which are not listed but which nevertheless have a certain local flavour and might be worth preserving either individually or as part of a group. Above and right: these two 19th century buildings are in Horsham.

In most towns there will be odd individual items in the street that have historial significance, such as this lock-up at Alton, right, or which are valuable as ornaments to the street and would be difficult to replace, left.

Buildings like this bank in Newark are substantial and valuable properties. In considering the character of a town they should be seen as permanent parts of the townscape, unlikely to be redeveloped.

Some buildings are worth keeping because of the visual contribution they make to a totally
changed setting. This pub in
Brighton, left, has a highly
decorative façade which, although of no real architectural
quality, might well be preserved
as part of a development scheme,
sketch below.

In many towns, the local character is not confined to
buildings; walls and railings, ramps and steps are
important as well. Above: street walls at Arundel.

Steps, Newcastle-on-Tyne.

The importance of setting

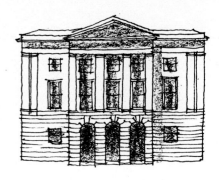

The setting of a building not only affects the way in which it can be seen, but also alters the apparent value and importance of the building itself.

Standing by itself, a building has no meaning other than that which comes from the intrinsic quality of its architecture—it has no context in which to function. Conservation will be concerned not only with buildings but also with their setting and its character.

It might be the formal focal point of a town square, left.

Or it might be merely an incidental part of the street scene, above. Right: situated on a bend, it becomes less an incident and more of a focal point.

28

You might find yourself looking up at it.
Or down at it, depending on the local topography,
below.

Surrounded tightly
by other buildings,
above, its qualities
are hidden until you
are almost upon it.

The scale of development around it gives it significance, above left, or reduces its importance, above
right.

It might be important to the town as a whole, below.

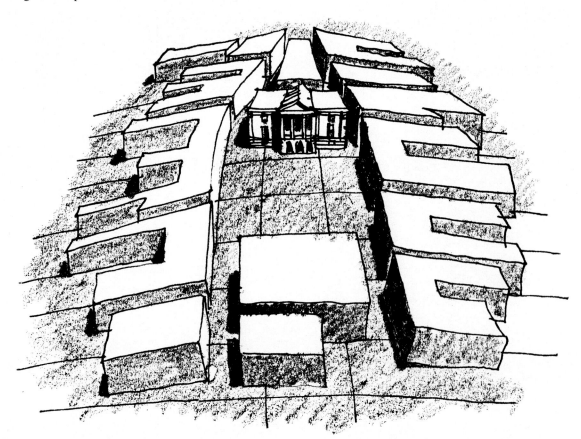

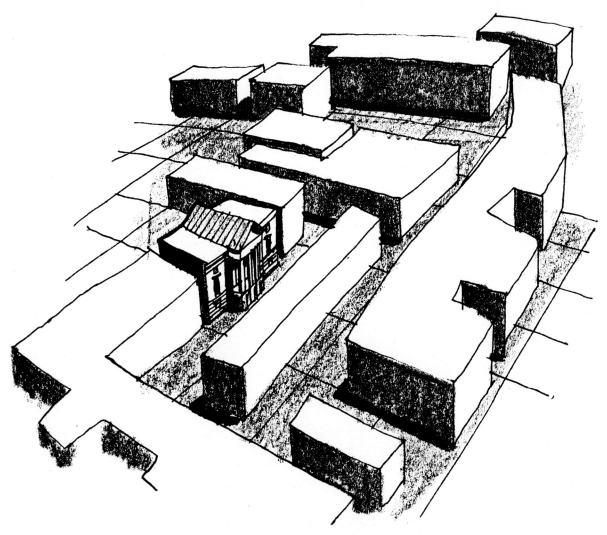

Or it might be only incidental to the town's total image.

organisation of spaces and an arrangement of buildings which *combines* as a whole. Furthermore, the total image of a town (its relationship to the countryside, its underlying land form, its archaeological layout) may be so powerful that it merits conservation on that one count alone if the town's real identity is to be maintained. The town's size and the number of people who live in it will also be constituent parts of its character.

So the scope is wide; it is even dangerously wide. With perhaps a few exceptions (some of our more formal towns such as Bath and Cheltenham) preservation in the restrictive sense and on such a wide scale could become hopelessly damaging to the life and prosperity of the town. And preservation depends upon prosperity.

The various levels of a town's character, from the quality of an individual building to its relationship with the surrounding countryside, need different

31

methods of approach if a realistic policy of conservation is to be achieved. Consideration of individual buildings, along with certain limited aspects of the townscape such as the dominance of a church spire in a street, can result in a clear-cut decision that preservation is desirable. Preservation in these cases creates (given a situation of economic viability) a nearly static situation allowing only for the essential work of internal modernisation, external repair and environmental improvement.

The approach to general visual qualities (the largest part of the townscape, that is) must be less rigid, to create a less static situation. The word preservation is no longer applicable. We are dealing with a visual environment which is continually subject to change. What matters is how, and where, change takes place. By recognising or observing the reasons why a town or parts of a town have a particular image or atmosphere we will not aim to preserve these qualities item by item, but to influence and direct development within a meaningful and sympathetic standard of townscape design, that maintains and encourages a feeling of local identity and the quality and interest of the setting of the historic buildings.

Conservation policies must therefore aim both to *preserve* the most valuable architectural aspects of our towns and *discipline* or *inspire* what is changing. The recognition of townscape as a guide to the design and siting of new development is the link of reconciliation between preservation and change.

In the diagram below, the identification of historic buildings and the assessment of townscape is shown as part of a visual and historic survey with parallel and complementary policy objectives or aims.

Assuming in broad terms we know what it is we want to conserve and we have some philosophy of approach, we must go on to examine the pressures that create the need for change and how they affect existing buildings and townscape.

It has already been said that a changing society, growing in numbers,

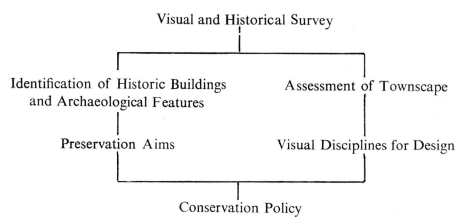

Visual and Historical Survey

Identification of Historic Buildings and Archaeological Features   Assessment of Townscape

Preservation Aims   Visual Disciplines for Design

Conservation Policy

32

creates the need for a changing environment. In any case that environment, in so far as it is part and parcel of the fabric of our towns, must be constantly renewed because the building materials of its fabric decay and wear out. But how extensive and real is the need for a changing environment? There are obviously areas where the environment is quite unsuitable for present-day use and it would be irresponsible to contemplate their retention in the future. Such are the nearly two million houses classed as slums which must be replaced. But the question can only be answered by examining the needs of society itself.

Can the idea of *town*, *city* or *village* (and these are at present the widest visual units of community identity) continue as a suitable physical reflection of the different types and sizes of community, the people who live there and their aspirations? With the individual ownership of cars (and the roads to go with them) or the most effective public transport facilities, shopping and work can be offered on a regional scale. Leisure activity is now available on a national and even an international scale: T.V. comes live from outer space.

Is the idea of *town* as an organic, self-contained unit outdated? Is it outdated, not only because the use of cars has choked up towns and made them inefficient, but also because as units towns no longer reflect a working organisation of society? It is at least feasible that individual small towns could disappear as centres of community activity. They could become mere housing estates to regional centres containing all the facilities we require.

Gordon Cullen, again in his book *Townscape*, says "there are advantages to be gained from the gathering together of people to form a town. A single family living in the country can scarcely hope to drop into a theatre, have a meal out or browse in a library, whereas the same family living in a town can enjoy these amenities. The little money that one family can afford is multiplied by thousands so a collective amenity is made possible". These are of course advantages which increase with the size of the community; the larger the community the more facilities it can support.

Separate towns have, however, certain advantages over conurbations; they allow ready access to countryside, they create the opportunity for a socially identifiable group of people to live together and know each other as a community. Within a city region and with a regional transportation system they can now be provided with minority amenities and facilities. There is no reason why such older towns should not maintain their separate identity within new regional structures. In fact, there seems every reason for the retention of individual towns (and the creation of new ones) rather than the acceptance of extended suburban sprawl in the Los Angeles sense. It is not now uncommon to hear the sprawl of many American cities accepted and praised—an acceptance born perhaps of the sense of our own inability to plan effectively the deployment of population growth.

I cannot conceal my own personal taste for small towns and their retention as such. My own home town is still small enough (23,000) to create a sense of belonging to a community with a separate identity. It lacks for example a professional theatre or specialised restaurants, and it has no art gallery, but these are obtainable 36 miles away, or forty-five minutes away by train, in London, or thirty-five minutes by car down the main road, in Brighton. It supports highly successful amateur theatrical productions, a civic society and a film society and countless other groups from fur and feather appreciation to the Mothers' Union. The town centre is a real meeting place.

If, then, we do accept the indefinite survival of individual and separate towns, more or less as we know them today (the Buchanan Report, *Traffic in Towns*, assumes that if compactness of population is maintained, there will still be towns broadly in the form we know them today) we must also accept that their internal organisation as units will change to accommodate changing local needs. Their townscape must respond accordingly.

If we are to discipline that response we must understand the nature of the visual and social effects those changes are having now and are likely to have in the future. The illustrations on pages 11–16 show a number of aspects of change and their visual consequences.

The close relationship between physical and social change has already been discussed. Change affects towns in two ways. Socially it is manifested in the need for new buildings and structures and the demand for services and amenities, and structurally it is manifested in the presence of decay, when the fabric of a town ages and begins to deteriorate and is no longer capable of efficient use.

Pressure for physical change directly reflects the growth of population, its structure and spending power and its desire for mobility. This growth will attract local, national and private investment, and it will in turn make demands on public resources. Where the population is not increasing, the situation is usually exactly the opposite—there is little growth in spending power and no attraction for investment; so there is less pressure for physical change. These conditions are the basis of economic viability.

The visible effect of physical change in these two situations of expansion or stagnation will be different and will affect different parts of towns. Where there is growth the town centres will come under increased pressure for redevelopment—pressure for building new roads or widening others, for providing car parks, new shops and offices. Owners of buildings and land will want to realise the increased value of their sites. Pressure will mount for the demolition of old buildings and their structural condition will begin to deteriorate as owners anticipate redevelopment. The appearance of the town as a whole will change as new development begins to spread out over the surrounding countryside.

34

In the second situation, where there is no population growth or perhaps only a slow rate of expansion, the pressure for development will not be so acute. There are obvious advantages for preservation under these conditions. The overall appearance of the town will remain much the same, the surrounding countryside will be preserved and the town's domestic scale maintained. The town centre will not attract investment so readily and trade will continue on a scale more suitable for the existing buildings: site values will not inflate so dramatically. There will of course be a need to accommodate extra traffic due to the normal rise in car ownership, while the lack of development projects may make it difficult to achieve even piecemeal improvements. The average age of the population may rise, and the lack of wider social structure will create little opportunity to maintain the older houses in full and useful occupation. Standards of repair and maintenance will consequently suffer. There will be a tendency for trade to gravitate to a few shops and correspondingly the need for secondary shopping will decline. Old buildings do, however, provide premises for activities which are not commercial or not profitable enough to pay the higher rents of new buildings; in a larger town these old buildings may prove to be a valuable asset. For example, small local industries can seldom afford the rents on new industrial estates, but find old buildings cheaper and often more adaptable.

Between these two extremes of rapid expansion and little or no growth are of course countless towns with varying degrees and types of pressure for change. Some, for example, where there is a tourist attraction, find themselves with a difficult problem in dealing with visitors' cars and coaches. A town in which there is no apparent reason for natural growth may find that the siting of a new town, or the rapid expansion of an old one near by, may bring an influx of commuters looking for a small town in which to live. Any conservation policy must take account of these differing pressures for change. It must work with them and use them or, more fundamentally, see that the pressures are altered.

The fabric of an existing town, its qualities of architecture and townscape, will have a ready-made capacity for carrying traffic and for absorbing new development, and once this capacity is exceeded, the town's character will be altered. Change can therefore be absorbed up to a certain point (assuming this is done sympathetically) and beyond that point must be diverted in some way. The alternative, which might well prove to be the only realistic one in some towns, is to change the identity completely, cutting off the town from its past.

If change is to be absorbed, areas or sites for change within the town must be chosen to create a sympathetic relationship with what is preserved (and this may mean selected piecemeal development within a comprehensive programme for environmental improvement). Where change is to be diverted, other towns must be selected to receive more than their normal share of development, or completely new settlements must be considered. A conservation policy for one town can therefore be formulated only within a wide planning framework. The demand for buildings, whether old or new, and consequently their economic viability, directly reflects the social structure of the town and its regional function. At present, conservation policy is seldom considered outside the immediate vicinity of an area of historic buildings.

Early assessments, however broad, should be made of conservation needs, so as to produce aims for testing against, and for compatibility with, other planning requirements at regional level. The assessment would set out to establish the effects of conservation on the future function of towns, villages or regional centres, and in reverse the likely effects of growth on conservation.

Town expansion (the expansion of an existing town to take overspill from another) has of course certain social advantages. There is an existing community structure that will benefit newcomers (give them some roots on which to thrive) and the expansion will make it possible to provide additional amenities for the existing population should they want them. But the cost of adapting an existing town for a sudden increase in population appears to be greater than that of starting afresh on a new settlement.

Where there is a large area containing a number of towns and villages worthy of extensive conservation, growth and development might be better concentrated in a new settlement or series of village settlements.

The task of drawing up a regional conservation policy will naturally be somewhat more complicated than simply choosing which towns to preserve and which to change. For example, many towns will already have proposals in the pipeline which cannot be halted. An old shopping centre might be decaying through lack of trade, but additional and more attractive shopping provision and a wider catchment area might bring back lost trade as an aid to preservation. The modernisation of existing services and the conversion of buildings will still be required to keep abreast of the needs of even a static population although the town is to be the subject of a strong conservation policy.

Running through all problems of conservation there is therefore the fundamental problem of population growth. The essence of the character of most towns is the town centre, embodying both the social and commercial life of the town. The number of people which that centre must serve—the size of population—will determine its ability to sustain a conservation policy. In reverse the town centre will, if its character is to be preserved, set a limit to population growth, a limit to the satisfaction of certain kinds of economic demand, and will determine the pattern of social structure or regional function.

36

Many people say that towns decay if their population ceases to expand. There are, of course, two kinds of population growth: immigrant growth (people moving in from outside) and natural growth (the excess of births over deaths). The first is to some extent controllable, and indeed it must be controlled if worthwhile conservation over whole areas is to succeed. The second is, in our society at any rate, impossible to control but is usually slower to take effect and consequently more acceptable. The resultant change in the fabric of the town is also more acceptable. Nevertheless, many towns have remained static in population terms and this does not necessarily mean that they decay.

Barnard Castle is a small, compact town in Durham which has remained almost static. Between 1956 and 1961 the population grew from 5,039 to 5,389. Between 1961 and 1966 the population decreased by 27 people to 5,362. This was largely due to the completion of work on a nearby reservoir and a run-down in the civilian personnel at an army camp. But the climate for conservation seems to have been right. There has been little threat either of redevelopment or from decay of the historic buildings. A delicate balance has been found.

In these towns that remain static and yet are able to preserve their fabric, the average age of the population goes up but their character changes. It changes in social class and in occupation.

These static towns, because they are often quiet, and still have an undisturbed atmosphere, attract wealthier commuters from nearby commercial centres, retired people and people looking for weekend accommodation. These three groups of people have a strong interest in retaining the identity of the place, its size and its quiet atmosphere. If evidence is needed one need only look at the membership of many civic or preservation societies and the location of those societies.

This new social structure offers a sure aid to conservation, though in other social terms a more mixed community may be more desirable. With an older age group there is, of course, no longer the same increase of births over deaths and the local population will need to be constantly topped up by people for whom this type of accommodation is suitable.

Two good examples of towns undergoing this change in social structure are Sandwich in Kent and Rye in Sussex. In their older parts both have experienced the take-over of quite small terraced houses (including those of no real architectural quality) by retired people and weekenders. The value of these properties has risen sharply—a clear guide to the demand. This reinforces the belief that there is something in the saying, "preservation for the rich, change for the poor".

There are of course those with a strong interest in expansion, none more obvious than the small shopkeeper, often well represented on the local council, who is probably having a hard time in competition with supermarkets and is not helped by the weekenders who are only with him for one shopping day. But an increase in population does not bring any guaranteed longterm advantage. Given a larger population, a supermarket will swoop in to mop up the extra trade, leaving the small shopkeeper worse off than he was before and the planner faced with yet another cry for further expansion.

Size and growth of population not only determine the pressure for change; the size of a place (the number of people who live there) is also an important factor in creating its identity. For example, a village is a village because of the small number of people who live there. Increase its size and it is no longer a village.

Many towns will not have a total image or character at all (though if we study them closely, probably more will have it than we imagine). Some will have quite small areas which might retain their identity within a radically changed framework. This will apply to the larger cities and certainly to the conurbations.

Where there is a large expansion of population there might be a need for radical changes in the distribution and location of land uses to achieve, for example, a sensible transport policy or to reduce the pressure on the existing town centre. The possibility of the conversion of an old shopping centre into residential or business use with new shopping on a completely new site is a solution which is often discussed. But it is difficult to imagine Ludlow and Shrewsbury, for example, changing in this way and yet still retaining their individual identity and character, quite apart from the prohibitive cost of such an operation. The character of these towns is

Preservation for the rich, change for the poor.

38

Size and function are the basic ingredients of character.
Obviously Broadway, in the Cotswolds, above, is different from a city centre, left. This is not only because the materials are different or that trees in one are commonplace and in the other occasional. The fabric of the two places; the buildings, the squares and their scale—represent different sizes of community, different activities and functions. Conservation will be concerned with maintaining these differences.

Conservation will be concerned with the relationship of the historic areas to other areas in the town. The character of Ludlow, above, is essentially derived from the siting on a hilltop of the commercial core of historic buildings. To change the relationship of the commercial core to other areas in the town would alter its significance as the focal point of the town's life.

essentially derived from the siting of their historic commercial centres on a hilltop. To change this would alter the significance of the central core as the focal point of a town's social life.

To sum up: an appraisal of conservation aims, covering desirable preservation standards and design aims in one town, must therefore be compatible with the economic and social functions of the region. These aims, as they are tested against other planning aims and regional requirements, will set broad targets for growth and conservation. Whilst there is at present no regional planning staff preparing such a policy, much can be achieved, and is being achieved, at sub-regional level by co-operation between planning authorities. In many cases a subregional conservation policy will often be sufficient.

In their review of the planning system, the Ministry of Housing and

Local Government's Planning Advisory Group Report (*The Future of Development Plans*, H.M.S.O. 1965)* stated in paragraph 144:

"The regional context (for local plans) will be set out in plans prepared by the Economic Planning Boards and Councils. These are likely to be primarily concerned with creating the conditions of economic growth in some regions and controlling the pace of growth in others, within the framework of national economic planning. As part of this process they will have to be concerned with physical planning issues which have regional significance, with the overall distribution of population and employment, green belt policy and any other limitations on growth in the conurbations."

Paragraph 36 states that the proposed county plans would, *inter alia*, "set the policy framework for development in towns and villages". And yet they would "provide, in the preparatory stages, a basis for consultation and negotiation with County District Councils, neighbouring planning authorities, regional authorities and Central Government on matters of common interest".

This sets out the method and framework within which conservation could be considered over wide levels of planning policy.

* The Planning Bill before Parliament when this book was written (1968) embodies the main proposals of the Planning Advisory Group's report for the reorganisation of the planning system.

II. PRINCIPLES OF CONSERVATION

Much has been written about the problems of preserving individual buildings in terms of structural and decorative condition, including the problems of conversion. Similarly much has been achieved by local authorities in schemes of conversion and repair using both public and private finance: there is no need to describe the application and working of those schemes here.

But underlying the detailed problems of preservation as they affect individual buildings, are a number of fundamental principles which ought to guide preservation as part of the whole process of planning a town.

These principles concern selection, economic viability and the definition of public and private sectors of action.

1. Selection

Despite the necessity to maintain the character of a town as a whole and sometimes its overall image or size, the total fabric of towns cannot be preserved brick by brick. As has been said, preservation in many ways needs change in order to be effective. So preservation must, therefore, to some degree be selective to make way for change.

One of the most difficult aspects of conservation is to decide on an order of priorities. Whereas the benefits of building shops or offices, for example, can be weighed in economic terms or in terms of convenience against building on alternative sites, no such precise value can be given to aesthetic alternatives. Although the cost of preserving one building can be weighed against the cost of preserving another, the choice between say preserving a good Victorian building or a good Georgian building with similar problems of maintenance and repair is an aesthetic choice, which is not quantifiable.

It will usually, therefore, prove necessary for the architect or historian to grade various aspects of a town's identity in an order of priority for conservation. The grading of these qualities becomes as much an aesthetic judgement as the appraisal of the qualities in the first place. The architect might, for example, define areas of historic buildings in order of importance or grade areas of countryside—defining those which are essential to the visual image of the town and those which are not quite so essential.

2. Restriction and Expansion

The need for a regional assessment of conservation aims has already been discussed; conservation in one town demanding increases in the growth of another. Where there is need for change the same balance of restriction and expansion must occur within towns. If one part of a town is to be preserved

42

then another part must be allocated for change. For example, where an existing high street would be spoilt by further development, new sites must be provided on which to build shops.

In identifying the opportunities for preservation we must also identify the opportunities for new development. To some extent this may be absorbed within an area of conservation, but in many cases the magnitude of change will demand new sites for development. In a town where there is a demand for high buildings, proposals to maintain the existing height of one area will only be practicable when another area in the town can be found in which high buildings are desirable. Similarly, if the traffic capacity in a street which is to be preserved has been reached, a new route must be found for the extra vehicles, or the use of vehicles restricted.

3. Efficient Use and Economic Viability

To be effective, conservation must be based on efficient use and economic viability. These two qualities are interdependent; the economic viability of a building depends upon the use to which it can be put. For a building to function efficiently it must not only be convenient to use but also capable of use at reasonable cost. It must not be too expensive to maintain in good condition and its situation must be suited to its use.

Just as the adequacy of the supply of electricty, gas and water helps to determine a building's value, the ease and safety by which it can be reached by vehicles or pedestrians also affects its value and efficiency. Likewise its situation will also determine whether it is quiet or noisy, pleasant or not so pleasant to live or work in. Its location and its consequent environment thus affect its use and its viability.

Therefore good environment, efficient use, and economic viability are essential for effective preservation. Whilst many forms of new development have these qualities, all too often older existing areas are expected to survive without them. The provision of these conditions does not, however, automatically ensure effective preservation.

Whatever the environment of a building it will remain empty unless there is a demand for the use of a structure of that type, in that particular part of a town, or in that particular town as opposed to another.

The efficient use of a building therefore requires either a ready-made demand or that a new demand should be created for it. This may well be a regional problem—a town with rows and rows of Regency terraces may well require a source of residents not to be found amongst the social structure of the town as it stands. The introduction of a commercial firm (or perhaps as has happened in several towns, a branch of the armed services) may provide the right income group to use the properties beneficially. A university may require accommodation for students and this can create a demand for flats in large houses or over shops.

Sympathetic conversion into smaller units of accommodation or a change from residential to office use may increase the demand for the buildings.

4. Priorities for Investment

A local authority must decide upon its priorities for investment and use of manpower in relation to that which can be expected from private resources.

To be successful, preservation will require the widest possible use of private investment. There will be a limited amount of investment available from local authorities and that must be applied to action which, because of its special powers, only the local authority can undertake effectively, and to action which will encourage private investment.

This will generally mean that local authorities should concentrate on environmental improvement, leaving the conversion, maintenance and repair of property as far as possible in the hands of private investment. This causes two main difficulties. First, improvement to the environment (providing alternative traffic routes, service roads or garaging for example) tends to raise site values as well as building values. A rise in site values can create pressure for redevelopment which is not conducive to preservation. Environmental improvement may, therefore, mean the accompanying use of preservation orders. Second, improvement to the environment is usually financially unproductive to the local authority unless the buildings to be preserved are also acquired by the authority, and unless some additional revenue can be found, such as an increase in rateable value, the local authority may be deterred from taking action. A town's programme of investment will be shared between both old and new development. But it should be remembered that preservation may need early assistance, as decay in older property or its environment, if not arrested quickly, can soon make a building unfit for use.

5. Public Relations

An informed public is essential for an effective Conservation Policy—it must, however, be informed before the event, not after. A statement of intent by the local authority can express its desire to preserve buildings, saying why they are architecturally valuable and what supporting action is proposed. A well-illustrated document showing the buildings and the qualities that are to be preserved can be produced from the survey material. Co-opting the local Civic or Historical Society will help to put the message across to owners, developers and the general public. Public meetings where policies are explained are an essential part of establishing a Conservation Policy.

The definition of areas where the preservation of buildings is to be the principal planning aim (Conservation Areas) is an essential public relations device. However, there are a number of dangers in defining these areas and

In many towns there are direct visual and social links with the past. At the Bull Ring in Birmingham, despite considerable redevelopment, a market still exists on the same spot as it has done for hundreds of years. Here is living evidence of a town's past. Above, the Bull Ring, in 1830, left, the Bull Ring today.

consequently it should be done with care. The greatest danger lies in the isolation of such areas from the organic form and structure of the town. To continue to have meaning, a Conservation Area must function and appear to function as an integral part of the town as a whole. New road schemes, for example, should avoid becoming barriers between the new parts of a town and the old parts.

Many people see conservation as a kind of setting-aside, perhaps converting buildings to residential use, painting them in a selection of fashionable colours, thinking apparently mainly of visitors and photographs. But if history is to have any significance today, and if there is to be a continuity with the past, conservation must be concerned with the maintenance of a living environment. Certainly some Conservation Areas need to be quiet and restful places, but others can only evoke their past by being bustling, lively places and part of the life of the local community.

There is great pleasure to be had in visiting a town and being able to see, for example, where Romans once walked or where the market has been held for centuries. But the pleasure is more intense if we can still walk where the Romans walked, or shop on the same site as the original market. This is surely more exciting than reading a plaque about it, or finding a piece of ancient wall preserved behind glass in the basement of an office block. The piece of city wall preserved in the London Wall Development to the north of St. Paul's, or the preservation on a roundabout of the Bargate in Southampton, succeed only in reducing the historic significance of the monuments.

Conservation Areas

A Conservation Area will usually be defined because of the presence of an overall architectural quality or historic associations. Those associations often give the area a significant historical and social relationship to the rest of the town. The siting of the Conservation Area in relation to other areas of the town will have established its physical and social importance, and changing the relationship can alter the significance of the area. So in considering Conservation Areas they must be seen in the context of the whole town both for historic and visual reasons and in order to provide a proper context in which to plan for conservation.

If we begin defining a Conservation Area by putting a ring round part or parts of a town where there are concentrations of historic buildings we shall arrive at very different kinds of Conservation Area from town to town, both in size and function. There can consequently be no standard Conservation Area. A town like Stamford for example is almost solid with listed buildings over a large part of its total area. Norwich has listed buildings scattered over a large central area, some in groups but most

Conservation areas will vary in size and function and contain anything from a small group of buildings to a whole town or village or a town centre. The town centre of Stratford upon Avon, above, is an obvious choice. Below left, the Causeway in Horsham: a group of buildings making up a small conservation area. The form and layout of adjoining streets might also be retained. Below right, Slaugham: a village conservation area.

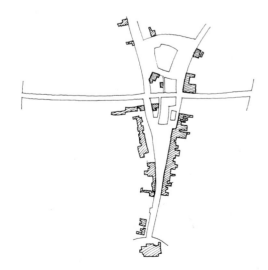

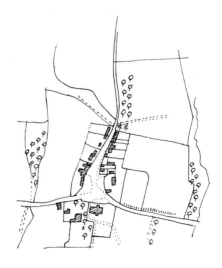

occurring individually. In the centre of Bristol there are nine small areas and one larger area with concentrations of historic buildings, as well as many individual listed buildings elsewhere. A city like Liverpool or a small town like Knaresborough has only a few listed buildings, but still needs a policy of conservation to retain its special identity and townscape.

We have defined conservation as being about both achieving effective preservation and the discipline of change. The term Conservation Area must therefore be taken to mean an area in which preservation will be a principal planning aim but in which some change, although small in scale, must nevertheless take place. This scale of change will include the occasional piecemeal redevelopment of buildings or the replacement of eyesores and the provision of garages and service roads, for example.

But in different types of area there will be different types of problems to be solved. In town centres large capacity car parks, service roads and other new development may be required to assist in preservation. The areas of action will vary considerably and the size of the Conservation Area, if it were to include this development, would no longer define just the concentration of listed buildings but would cover a much wider area, quite out of the scope of a Conservation Area. Nevertheless new development would need to be seen in physical and visual relationship to the Conservation Area.

There are many reasons why the area of planning action would need to be larger than the Conservation Area: for example in order to achieve a better standard of environment, additional houses may have to be added to the area to make improvement worth while. A by-pass for through traffic or a service road to local shops, may then become economically possible. Additional high-density housing adjoining a group of shops of historic value may be required to sustain the properties and give a boost to trade.

There will sometimes be a need to create an area which is more self-supporting. Take as an example a group of houses which is detached from other groups and perhaps has no local shopping facilities, no readily accessible open space and few private garages. Where the existing houses are deteriorating or dropping in value because of a lack of these amenities, the addition of more housing may make it practicable for the amenities to be provided. Occasionally two small groups of buildings that are worth preserving might be joined by new development to make a complete entity.

Thus the function, size and problems of Conservation Areas will vary considerably. But if public statements are to have any meaning, and are to be clearly understood, both locally and nationally, it must be generally agreed what such areas are for and what their definition implies. In order to be generally applicable the definition must be simple and quite distinct from other terms used in town planning. As has been said before, where preservation is concerned, public participation and understanding are essential. The term Conservation Area should, therefore, be used quite

48

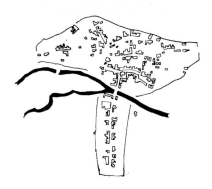

Three more possible conservation areas: above, Stamford—the whole of the old town within the walls and St. Martin's in the south: in Norwich, right, the whole of a large city centre is enclosed by the line of the old walls. The centre may contain a number of conservation areas but the whole complex needs to be considered as one unit in design terms. Below, Bristol—several unrelated conservation areas in a radically changing city centre. Scale in all three pictures is the same.

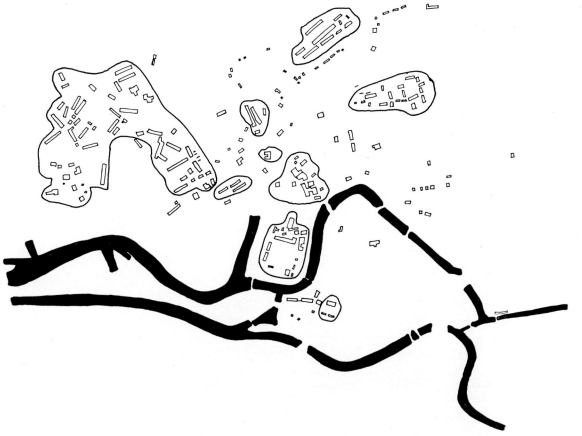

separately from other planning terms; it is not in itself an instrument of planning technique as is an Environmental Area or an Action Area. A Conservation Area only defines an aim and a set of problems. Supporting policies will be required to back the definition.

The designation of a Conservation Area is a public statement of intent by the local authority, rather similar to the listing of buildings by the Ministry of Housing. Listing does not, by itself, preserve a building. It is however a public warning and a statement of an aim. The designation of an area is different from the listing of a building in that it is also an assurance of support by the local authority. It is a warning that the local authority intends a whole area to be the subject of conservation; that preservation orders will almost certainly be made on the majority of listed buildings if the need arises*; that strict control of clutter will be enforced (the Conservation Area may coincide with an Area of Special Advertisement Control); that, where necessary, tree preservation orders will be made; that new development must be visually and functionally suited to the aims of conservation; that where necessary planning control will be extended by Article 4 directions.

The local authority can expect to be backed more effectively in the future on appeal cases in Conservation Areas where aesthetic grounds are given for refusal of planning permission. As a general rule no outline planning permissions should be given in a Conservation Area and elevational details should be seen before planning permission is granted.

It has been said that the definition of a Conservation Area is an assurance and that this will help in fostering good will: it is an indication that the local authority will take supporting planning action to create a high standard of environment (such action being, in effect, programmed by the identification of Action Areas). It is an assurance also that the local authority will, wherever necessary back the preservation of buildings with whatever financial help it can give under the Local Authorities' (Historic Buildings) Act 1962. The local authority may work with the Historic Buildings Council to implement grants in a Town Scheme, and will also encourage applications for improvement grants for internal modernisation —construction of bathrooms, provision of hot water supply, etc. It may relax regulations when applications are received for new development or conversion within the area.

The delegation of planning powers to District Councils may need to be reviewed. There are clearly many ways in which a local planning authority can toughen up its action on both the preservation of historic buildings and the control of change. The Civic Amenities Act gives stronger powers

* The new planning legislation in effect abolishes the preservation order. Before demolition or alteration of a listed building can take place a grant of "listed building consent" will be required.

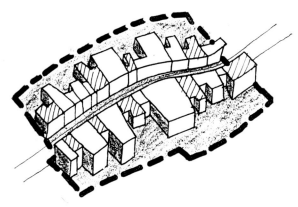

Extent of conservation areas

The conservation area will be concerned with the setting of historic buildings and the definition of an area of identity or completeness. Assessment of identity areas is described on pages 130–7. By thinking in terms of an area, rather than a number of individual buildings, we are identifying an entity, as the examples here and on pages 53 and 55 show. Historic buildings are indicated by shading. This area may already be viable and visually complete, or may need to be strengthened by the addition of some new development in areas of opportunity.

The extent of the area may be determined by the line of a street, left.

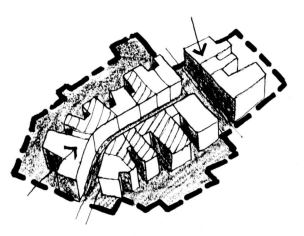

It may also be determined by the buildings enclosing the street and stopping off the views out.

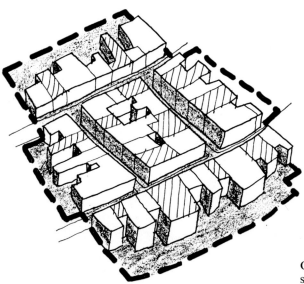

Or it may be determined by the pattern of several streets.

51

primarily in respect of listed buildings. It should, however, be remembered that conservation needs public goodwill and this is unlikely to be forthcoming under the early announcement of many extra controls.

The method of designating Conservation Areas is laid down in the Civic Amenities Act 1967. There is no formal procedure other than the publication of the designation in the *London Gazette* and at least one local newspaper. The Minister of Housing and Local Government has only to be notified of the designation and he in no way confirms or approves it.

If, in the opinion of the Local Planning Authority a planning application affects the character of the area, details of applications must be published in a local newspaper and be available for inspection by the public for twenty-one days.

The designation must define the Conservation Area accurately and a map of the area will usually be essential. The success of the Conservation Area will depend initially on the area being accurately defined. The boundary of the Area should be drawn to define which buildings and sites are involved in conservation. The owners of property will want to know whether they are affected or not. A Conservation Area should therefore define those buildings which ought to be preserved and those sites which, if developed, will be the subject of Conservation Design Policies.

A Conservation Area will include sites for minor local improvements or redevelopment but will generally be taken to imply that decisions on the future of individual buildings will be weighted in favour of preservation. In most cases the area will be decided, not simply on the siting of listed buildings, but on the setting of those buildings and the need to protect a visual entity or identity area (see illustrations on pages 51, 53 and 55).

In larger towns where considerable change is expected, Design Policies will also need to cover areas adjoining the Conservation Area, but which could in no sense be taken to be concerned with actual conservation. The Conservation Area will therefore also have influence over neighbouring sites. A local authority may, if necessary, refuse a planning application in a Conservation Area on the grounds that it is aesthetically unsuitable to the area. It might also refuse an application on a site adjoining a Conservation Area, or where development would be visible from the Area, justifying the refusal by the detrimental effect of the application on the neighbouring Conservation Area. A High Buildings Policy which involves the protection of the Conservation Area might be implemented in this way.

The centre of cities such as York or Norwich, where considerable change has already taken place and much more will be needed to enable the city centre to work efficiently, will probably therefore include a number of Conservation Areas. The design and redevelopment of the whole central area, perhaps within the line of the city walls, will need careful consideration in relation to the Conservation Areas themselves, and the total

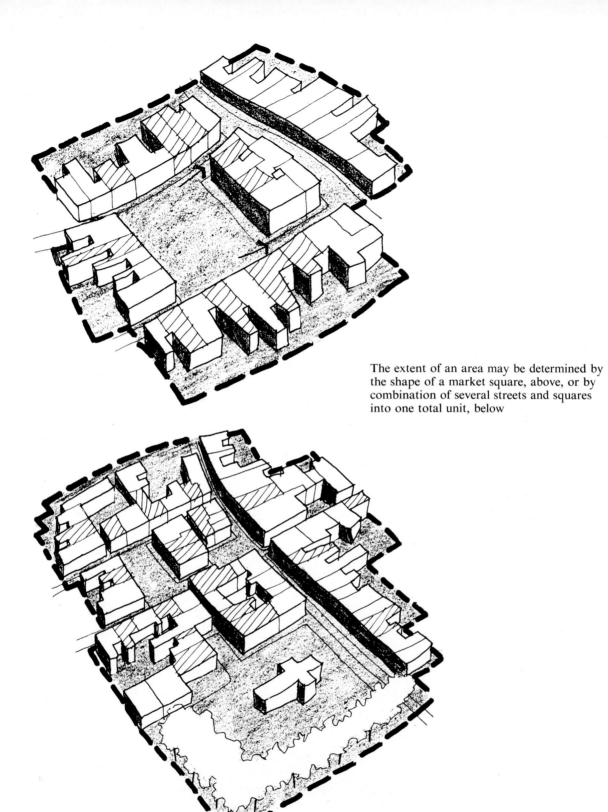

The extent of an area may be determined by the shape of a market square, above, or by combination of several streets and squares into one total unit, below

53

structural concept of the whole town centre. It is conceivable that the whole area of such city centres should be considered as Conservation Areas. However, this may well diminish its public impact as an area in which the preservation of historic buildings will be the principal aim. The inclusion within the Conservation Areas of areas where large-scale redevelopment will take place should be avoided wherever possible.

The designation of an area can be approached in two ways. It may be designated after it appears to the Local Planning Authority that it is fully practical, or it may be designated solely on the basis of the character of the area regardless of feasibility.

To designate an area without first being sure that it can in fact be maintained does, in the event of cancellation or failure, make a bad public impression and may affect the credibility of other Conservation Areas. On the other hand, not to define the area may well cause the area to decay through lack of public awareness.

It has been said that a Conservation Area is largely a statement of aims or intent. It is not, by itself, a proposal for specific action. Again it is similar to the listing of buildings. Listing is rightly carried out regardless of the feasibility of preservation—it identifies a desirable aim.

If there is no way of achieving even a degree of conservation then it would be pointless and bad for public relations to designate the area. But there are few areas which are in such a position and the benefits of a public statement of intent will positively aid conservation in terms of public confidence and enthusiasm.

Conservation schemes will be worked out as part of the normal planning policy of the town as a whole. The Structure Maps and local plans including Town Centre Maps will take account of the conservation aims. Two principal planning devices will affect the detailed implementation of conservation—first the Action Area, and second, the Environmental Area.

Action Areas

The Planning Advisory Group's Report recommended that Urban and County Plans should identify Action Areas, and in paragraph 44, sections 1 and 3, the main purposes of identifying Action Areas were defined as:

"1. to bring to the notice of the Minister and the public the principal features of the plan which it is intended to implement during the initial ten years or so, and thus to give greater depth and reality to the plan . . .
3. to identify the main areas which will require to be planned as a whole and in detail and to provide a basis for the preparation of more detailed proposals as a guide to developers and as a means of co-ordinating public and private development activities."

Conservation Areas, by definition, do not require comprehensive re-

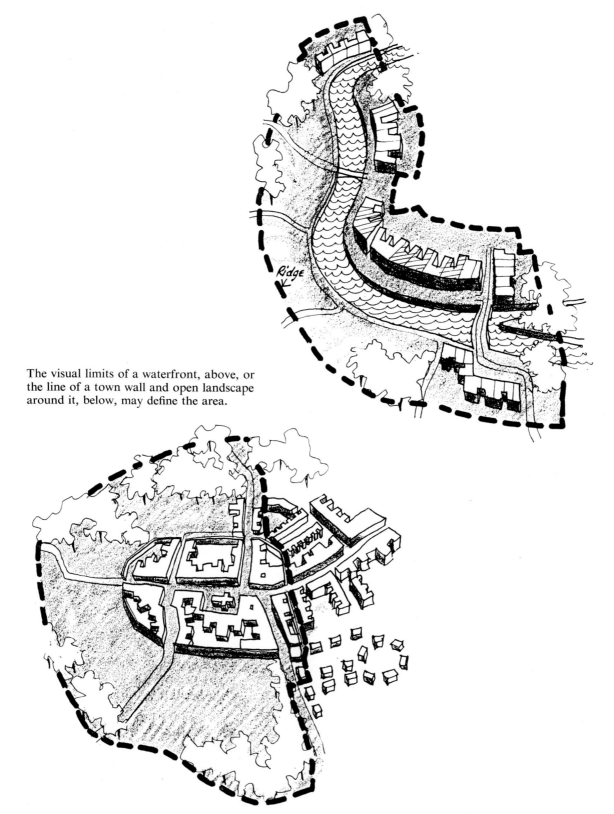

The visual limits of a waterfront, above, or
the line of a town wall and open landscape
around it, below, may define the area.

Ridge

55

development and the P.A.G. report went on to say that the term Comprehensive Development Area was not apt as a means of describing planning areas that are to be comprehensively improved as distinct from areas to be developed or redeveloped. By this definition a Conservation Area could clearly include or coincide with an Action Area that ought to be considered comprehensively. As has been suggested, in many towns the Conservation Area could well be the whole town centre or a very large part of it. Where there is a large Conservation Area it might contain several Action Areas; the Action Areas being used mainly as a programming device.

Environmental Areas

There is also another term in current planning use, which will be important to the Conservation Area. This is the Environmental Area; an area from which all extraneous traffic is removed. This might coincide with the boundaries of a Conservation Area or it might contain several small areas of historic buildings. A large Conservation Area might contain a number of Environmental Areas. The smaller the town, the more likely it is that an Environmental Area will coincide with the boundaries of the historic core of the town.

The Environmental Area may be the structural unit of town character in the future and could be the key to the maintenance of the completeness of the overall form and organic structure of towns. Environmental Areas would be chosen, among other things, from among areas which have a total architectural identity or a particular activity.

III. PLANNING FOR CONSERVATION

In drawing up policies and in physically planning for conservation, the conservation aims must first be tested for feasibility and compatibility with other planning aims. They must be seen to be feasible in the sense that the cost of preserving a building will not prove to be impossible to meet, either privately or publicly, and they must be compatible with other planning aims in the sense that where change is essential to implement a regional pattern of growth or solve local environmental problems, it is not unduly hindered or curtailed. So before drawing up planning schemes for conservation there must be an examination of the likely consequences.

Surveys associated with particular planning aims, to establish for example the condition of buildings or the quality of agricultural land, will be required to test the feasibility of conservation proposals (these are outlined on Chart 1, page 226). The list is not definitive and may vary from town to town.

There are two parallel levels of testing; first in relation to other local planning aims and second, in relation to needs for regional growth (outlined on Chart 2).

When these tests are completed (and they may vary in detail and content from town to town) the conservation aims may need to be adjusted. The next step is to decide the aims that can be achieved on the ground. This may again reveal need for adjustment. Some of the detailed problems and solutions involved in drawing up planning schemes for conservation are discussed under the headings below; first Central Areas, then Residential Areas, followed by Individual Historic Buildings and Groups of Buildings.

Central Areas

The layout of most old town centres is based on their original core of streets and property boundaries. In the eighteenth and nineteenth centuries the buildings were often remodelled or rebuilt but the pattern of the streets was seldom changed. Consequently the centres of our towns, designed originally for the pedestrian and the horse, are now creaking and splitting under the strain of modern traffic. Out of this situation comes one hopeful possibility. With the now general acceptance of the pedestrian precinct as a desirable planning aim, the old scale of human movement, for which the streets were designed, again comes into its own. But only certain streets may become pedestrian precincts and these will be mostly in the principal shopping areas, and even this is likely to be part of a fairly long-term programme.

Many streets will be able to go on carrying traffic and pedestrians. It should be remembered that the removal of all traffic over an extensive area

57

may inadvertently destroy much of the area's visual vitality, though this is obviously a matter of selection and degree.

It is curious how traffic has, despite its inconvenience and unpleasantness in the context of the urban environment, become something of a symbol of vitality. Many shopkeepers, for example, are still convinced that the removal of passing traffic will somehow cause a loss of trade, despite existing parking restrictions which prohibit door-step parking.

A display of folk dancing was given on the forecourt of St. Paul's Cathedral during May, 1967. The noise and fumes of passing traffic was almost unbearable and the space restricted. There is a new, much larger, pedestrian piazza no more than a hundred yards away almost empty. The forecourt has vitality and historic associations. Lots of people pass in cars and on foot. The piazza has no vitality and fewer people passing by. There is a lesson here for all pedestrian areas; they need to be compact, wind-proof and surrounded by many different uses with ample ground-floor shop frontage and with many people passing through. Large areas of pedestrian precinct may well work against conservation if their appearance is dull, monotonous and empty.

The short-term traffic proposals for a town centre will be all-important to conservation. Piecemeal proposals to accommodate traffic which will result in widening and straightening streets, should be avoided wherever possible, at least until a full assessment has been made of the long-term proposals. Street widening, by piecemeal setting back as and when properties are redeveloped, without any other reason than that it might one day be useful, has been recognised for years as a disastrous policy, yet it is still practised. There may be a case in some towns for temporary acceptance of some degree of congestion in order that interim road improvement schemes may be avoided.

Traffic management techniques will need to be employed as a holding action to stave off more drastic short-term measures until the long-term measures, including the provision of a road network over the town as a whole, can be effected.

Restriction of on-street parking will probably be essential to avoid widening or straightening streets. Cars must of course be parked somewhere if a shopping centre is to thrive, and the use of temporary sites for parking can often be phased with the clearance of land for future development. New permanent off-street car parks will be an early necessity.

Where on-street parking is restricted within the town centre, care should be taken to see that cars are not then parked in surrounding residential areas, particularly when these contain historic buildings where the environment must be especially protected. Parking in these residential areas may reduce the value of buildings and consequently cause early demolition. Restriction on parking in the town centre may therefore require

58

accompanying restriction on parking in neighbouring residential areas.

Restriction on parking or vehicle movement is only one side of the coin. The environmental capacity* of streets will set a limit on the absorption of both moving and parked vehicles. But in a Conservation Area as in any other form of development, people must be able to reach the buildings easily and conveniently, and the shops must be capable of easy servicing.

Public transport must play an increasingly important part in reducing private vehicle movement in older towns, and new methods of servicing shops and other buildings (for example by electric trucks centred on goods distribution centres) must be found.

Through traffic, if it is heavy, will need to be routed on to a by-pass at an early date. Many towns will find that a new local road system to the town centre can be designed to carry through traffic as a short-term measure until it can be by-passed at a later date (this may however prolong the time before the by-pass is constructed). Perhaps one of the most urgent problems affecting our older towns is the elimination of traffic passing through or across the historic core of the town centre as a short cut from one residential area to another, to places of work on the far side of the town, or traffic passing through the town with origin and destination outside. Many towns will find the diversion of this traffic a priority of conservation and amenity must soon be a stronger element in the determination of road programmes.

The introduction of one-way working for traffic has proved successful for most towns as an interim measure—one which enables the local authority to maintain the existing qualities of the town until a new road scheme can be implemented. One-way working can also, in some cases, provide a more permanent solution.

It must be remembered that a new development scheme, which by itself may do little architectural harm to the character of a town, can attract additional traffic, causing chaos in the neighbouring older parts of the town.

It has already been said that the conservation of the character of an area will define the area's capacity to carry traffic or to absorb development in that area. There are two principal aspects of new large-scale development that must be considered in relation to conservation: first, the siting of this development and its economic relationship to what is to be preserved, and second, the design and appearance of that development. The latter is dealt with in the section beginning on page 172 on the Design of Infilling.

Comprehensive development has almost become a catch phrase for town centres, but it is obviously inconsistent with a Conservation Area which covers a large part of a town centre. A more delicate urban surgery is

* When the stationary and moving traffic in a street exceeds the environmental capacity, the amenity and safety of the street deteriorate.

required. This does not mean that development can be considered piecemeal —a town centre must still be considered comprehensively if not redeveloped comprehensively. New road systems for example will naturally require a comprehensive approach.

If a town's population is to expand (the degree of expansion having been tested and established on a regional basis), additional shops, particularly the larger supermarkets and offices, must be provided to correspond to the increase of population. Multi-storey car parks, bowling alleys or a new civic centre may all be required as the population grows to support them. It has been suggested from time to time that where there is pressure for redevelopment in an old town centre, the construction of these new large-scale buildings away from existing buildings (in another part of the town or as an out of town centre) would preserve the scale and setting of the existing streets.

In a very large town or a town which is to expand considerably this may succeed. But whilst there is a strong aesthetic advantage in this and proposals of this sort may divert the pressures for new roads and car parks away from the town centre, they will also divert the trade upon which the smaller establishments rely. Under these conditions older shops will not survive and consequently the buildings which they occupy will deteriorate. This will not therefore, in the long run, achieve effective preservation. New development will almost certainly need to be integrated within the existing town centre (see also pages 40 and 137 Ludlow/Shrewsbury).

A large city or part of a conurbation may be able to divert one kind of trade—perhaps the multiple stores and supermarkets—to new sites, whereas the existing shops can still flourish on the demand for local and specialised trading. This will not apply to smaller towns where there is not likely to be a large enough demand for such shops.

Where new development must adjoin existing small-scale development the problem of the trading relationships between one and the other becomes critical. Each must be able to benefit from the presence of the other.

The existing pattern of shopping facilities will usually consist of smaller supermarkets and chain stores and a considerable number of old family businesses which contribute a great deal to the local identity.

A group of shops clearly requires a good trading position as a basis for economic viability. A new supermarket will not be attracted to a site which is cut off from the main pedestrian flows to and from the carparks or buses, and existing shops need the same consideration. The existing shops will suffer financially too if they are divorced from the undoubted trading attraction of the supermarket. The flow of pedestrians must therefore be designed to afford the maximum benefit to both existing and new shops. The diagrams opposite illustrate this point.

One of the main problems in preserving buildings used as shops is the

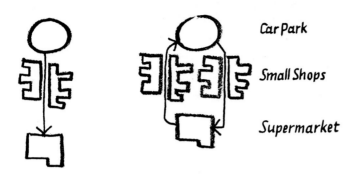

Car Park

Small Shops

Supermarket

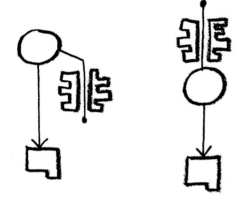

The relationship of new development to old, and particularly the movement of pedestrians between the two, will affect the economic viability of the buildings to be preserved. Above, layout beneficial to the conservation of a number of small shops. Left, layout detrimental to the conservation of small shops.

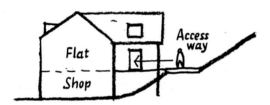

Flat

Shop

Access way

Pedestrian access from the rear to make upper floors more attractive in use.

frequent presence of two or three upper floors which are unused. These produce no rents which might otherwise help to maintain and repair the fabric of the old building. Shop owners often regard tenants of upper floors as a poor investment and inconvenient to both the shopkeeper and the tenant.

The close control of the lease of land for shop development and restriction on conversion of residential property into shops will put an economic premium on existing shop premises, although this does not serve the cause of preservation if pressure for redevelopment grows. The use of first-floor sales space should be encouraged wherever possible.

Planning and Building Regulations applications for conversion should be treated generously. Too rigid insistence upon normal floor heights, window openings and stair dimensions can deter conversion schemes. Local authorities have the power to waive Building Regulations where they think necessary, except where structural stability and fire regulations are concerned (these can only be waived by the Ministry of Housing on appeal). First-floor pedestrian access from the rear might be obtained where existing buildings are to adjoin new development. Sloping sites are an asset here.

The conversion of existing shopping streets to pedestrian ways creates a better environment, which may in turn lead to a bigger demand for living and office accommodation over shops. A policy to encourage the use of living accommodation in the town centre will only succeed if suitable open space, schools and other amenities are nearby. But the pleasures of living there can be considerable and, with good publicity on the part of the Council, such a policy can prove attractive. Furthermore a town centre which is inhabited is a much more lively place, particularly at night. People living over shops also bring a welcome convenience trade to the smaller shop-keeper.

Where rear access is provided, private parking facilities can usually be obtained within the curtilage of the property, on land which may otherwise remain unused. This will again make it more attractive for small office or residential use to be reinstated in upper floors with separate access away from the shopping streets.

Most of the old towns still have small shops with elongated sites which were once back gardens. These old gardens often occupy a large part of the town centre. Where they still exist they are often an important part of local identity, glimpsed from alleyways and side roads. They also encourage town-centre living and should not be discarded lightly. They can, however, often absorb excess shopping demand, thus avoiding new areas of development away from the existing shops. Four ways of making use of back land in an area where there is a demand for extra shops are shown overleaf. Historic buildings are retained in the main street.

In some cases, the amalgamation of a number of properties could provide the opportunity for the conversion of separate first-floor accommodation over several units into quite large residential or office properties.

Where a small existing town is to become part of an expanded town or new town (other towns having been selected for major conservation) a new shopping centre might well be built some distance away, leaving the old shops isolated from the new primary trading area. This may mean a substantial drop in trade and bring with it the closure of many small businesses and probably the slow decay of the historic buildings.

If the buildings are to be preserved, two courses are open to the planning authority. The shops might become the centre for a neighbourhood area.

A narrow frontage, left, often hides an extensive plot of land, below.

63

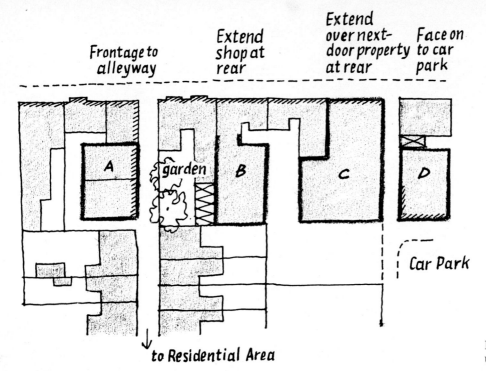

Frontage to alleyway

Extend shop at rear

Extend over next-door property at rear

Face on to car park

A

garden B

C

D

Car Park

to Residential Area

Four ways of making use of back land.

This might save some buildings, although not necessarily the most architecturally desirable, but the amount of trade would still be small and confined to local secondary shopping only. Alternatively the use of buildings could be changed by conversion; a majority of the shops being converted to houses, flats or offices. This would usually require public ownership but might be done as a co-operative effort. It would certainly be expensive. By announcing and implementing the scheme at an early stage the structural and decorative deterioration of the buildings can be prevented and the burden of the loss of trade to the shopkeepers could be eased. The visual and topographical consequences of this course of action were discussed earlier on pages 38 and 40.

Residential areas

The older residential areas are usually situated in the inner parts of the town, nearest the town centre, so that preservation is immediately important if only to reverse the trend towards living further away from town centres. It is also important to stop the drift of shops into the residential areas on the edges of the town centre. The more people live near their work, shops or offices, the less peak-hour traffic movement there is across the town. Where old houses can still be conveniently inhabited, they can play a considerable part in maintaining and increasing the variety of a town's total housing stock.

At the outset, having identified the buildings that warrant preservation, a number of fundamental questions must be asked. Firstly, who is to live in the houses? There is little hope of preserving buildings because of their architectural importance if they offer accommodation either too large or too small, or too expensive for the social structure of the community.

If the buildings are to be preserved, can they be divided into small units or can the existing properties be amalgamated to make larger ones for which there is a greater demand? This will depend upon two factors; the financial and structural suitability for conversion and the willingness of owners to carry out the work. The Council may need to carry out the work itself or again perhaps in co-operation with the owners by offering grants, improving the environment or working with a housing association. The local authority must assess whether the continual cost of maintenance, restoration and repair after conservation will be so high that standards will not be kept up and the consequent drain on public and private re-sources will be too great.

The same environmental problems will occur in assessing traffic capacity in a residential area as they do in a town centre.

Obviously fundamental environmental changes cannot be made over-night, neither will there be sufficient funds to achieve all that must be done to create the right conditions for long-term preservation. Priorities for improvement for all types of housing areas must be established, and phasing of proposals lined up with those over the town as a whole. Due weight should be given to the needs of Conservation Areas.

The standard to which the environment must be improved will be deter-mined to a large extent by the use to which the buildings can be put. For example, to take an extreme case, a group of eighteenth-century houses perhaps too big for present-day needs and situated on the side of a main road carrying heavy traffic night and day, may easily fall into disrepair. The inconvenience of living in them and the bad conditions of traffic noise and fumes make them difficult to let at an economic rent. This will dis-courage the owners from converting the property into suitable smaller units. It must be decided if and how the environmental conditions can be changed or improved.

It should not be forgotten that the introduction of double glazing and even air conditioning can soften the effects of a poor external environment.

A sufficient standard might be reached by a simple device such as a wall or embankment or tree planting. These might be used as short-term measures before a new road network or external by-pass is constructed which would remove the traffic altogether. If short-term improvments are accompanied by definite proposals for action on the part of the local authority, to incorporate the building in an Environmental Area within a specific time, confidence in the historic building may well be renewed (the definition of a Conservation Area with an associated Action Area promising early attention will be an advantage). If the environmental standard cannot be improved, permanent changes of use may make the buildings a better investment.

Changes of use can coincide with the introduction of short- and long-term measures for improving the environment. Perhaps in the short-term, before through traffic can be by-passed and taken out of the road altogether, the buildings might be suitable for office use where the acceptance of noise levels might be higher and where noise at night does not matter. This would largely depend upon the ease with which the buildings can be converted and perhaps at a later date revert to their original residential use. Residential use may be reinstated if the old houses are eventually to form part of a residential area.

By encouraging the construction of buildings in the surrounding area to a similar category of use or a compatible use, the older buildings are more likely to be retained in a sympathetic setting. Whatever decisions are taken, the main theme will be to maintain the economic viability of the existing building structure to resist pressure for redevelopment.

As with priorities for environmental improvement, changes of use must also be programmed with land use proposals for the whole town. For example, allowing office accommodation to replace residential uses will absorb some of the demand for new office development, but on the other hand a new scheme for offices could remove the possibility of achieving effective preservation by a change to office use in some existing houses. Conservation must therefore be supported by a suitable land-use policy for the town as a whole.

Unfavourable neighbouring uses such as factories or breweries can cause fumes and noise and unsightly views from residential property. The traffic generated can also cause a depression in local property values. In time, consideration might be given to resiting these undesirable neighbours, but a council can often improve the conditions in co-operation with the firm concerned. Modernisation of equipment can soften the effect of noise and fumes; screening by fences, walls and trees can reduce the visual intrusion. We should, of course, not forget that diversity also helps to create local identity.

In considering the environment of historic buildings the value of surrounding development must also be considered. An area of low-cost housing can result in the deterioration of more expensive historic buildings near by. New development on adjoining sites may well have to be closely related to the value of the existing historic buildings and the social class of the occupants. Co-operation with local firms in accommodating employees, with other local authority departments, or universities who have need for accommodation for staff and students, helps to make new uses for old

A small chapel incorporated into a school as a library.

buildings. For instance a welfare department may find a small group of houses suitable for elderly people.

Individual Historic Buildings and Groups of Buildings

Not every historic building or group of buildings will come conveniently within a Conservation Area. There are always occasional groups of buildings, perhaps consisting of four or five residential properties, situated away from the main areas of conservation. These will often be small cottages sometimes built as a terrace by the side of a main road. Road realignment is unlikely to be worth while to create a more pleasant environment. In this case they may be incorporated into the layout of new residential areas and the environment may be improved accordingly.

The larger individual properties are often the grandest architecture a town possesses—the family seat of the squire, the church for which there is no congregation, the corn exchange or warehouse without any goods. How can such buildings be retained when they provide the sort of accommodation which is now no use as it is and invariably difficult to convert?

Clearly some, such as churches or a corn exchange, because of their original civic purpose as a place of assembly, are more easily adapted to modern needs of a similar kind. They can sometimes be used for art galleries, museums or halls for public meetings. Additional floors can sometimes be inserted if required.

Some buildings which stand on larger, more open sites, may be incorporated into new development. The corn exchange might become the assembly hall of a school or part of a youth club; the old house provide the administrative part of a hospital or the small units of accommodation for a community centre; an old warehouse can be converted to light industrial use or provide office accommodation. Where new schemes are to incorporate old buildings the juxtaposition of the new with the old will be critical from an architectural point of view. Decisions must be taken on the visual part that the older building is to play in the total design, and it will often be possible to use the old building as the focal point of the development.

The identification of what to preserve and the policies and planning schemes that are needed will only answer part of the problem of the preservation of historic buildings. Much of the success of a preservation policy will depend upon the skill with which buildings are restored and maintained or converted to different uses. In many cases there will be a need for grants towards the upkeep of the buildings, and in most towns a detailed survey will be required of the condition of buildings and the requirements for repair and maintenance.

Where small buildings need restoration and repair, the larger the contract and the greater the number of buildings covered, the more reasonable the cost of conversion and restoration will usually be. Where properties have many different owners the council might help to initiate bulk contracts which could be financially beneficial.

The restoration of buildings of architectural and historic interest and their maintenance must be under the supervision of an architect or surveyor with special skills in this direction. Financial help may be needed with professional fees. A council should consider drawing up a list of such specialists and contractors which it could make available to assist householders. Where there is a continuous call for this type of advice, a committee of advisers could be set up. Responsibility for planning and carrying out schemes should be clearly defined between the various departments of a council. Each department should be informed of the part it has to play.

There are a number of sources of financial help for historic buildings. Under the Local Authorities (Historic Buildings) Act 1962, local authorities are empowered to make grants towards repair and maintenance. The

The office development for *The Economist*, by Alison
and Peter Smithson, contrasts with a building in St.
James's Street, using it as a focal point.

Whitehall Court,
London, was used as
a backdrop to the
Festival of Britain
1951.

Where an old build-
ing with a lot of fine
detail is close to new
buildings, a contrast
is usually most effec-
tive. The simplicity
and form of the
Royal College of
Physicians, by Denys
Lasdun, emphasises
the intricacy of a
Nash house near
Regents Park, Lon-
don.

Environmental improvement by tree planting, walls
and embankments.

Historic Buildings Council makes grants towards nationally important
historic buildings and also operates town schemes where buildings are considered for grants over a specific area rather than individually. This might
increasingly apply to Conservation Areas.

Some County Councils have set up Preservation Trusts where the County
and District Councils combine with private individuals or local societies to
set up a fund from which grants are made. This so far applies only to a
small number of counties—including Hertfordshire, Nottinghamshire,
Wiltshire and Kent. A number of private trusts also exist that will occasionally make grants towards the restoration of historic buildings. It should
not be forgotten that improvement grants apply to historic buildings as well
as other old buildings.

To assist in restoration and maintenance the council can provide a useful
service by salvaging old materials from buildings being demolished. Bricks,
tiles, paving slabs, stone setts, cast-iron bollards or lamps can all be stored
for eventual reuse; occasionally an offer of suitable building material can
be made to a householder by a Preservation Trust. A council may find it
worth while to undertake demolition work itself to ensure that materials
are not unnecessarily damaged.

Improvement in the environment will involve not only major works such
as the easing of traffic conditions or the provision of garages and service
roads, but also tidying up and rationalising street furniture, such as street

lighting, bus shelters and litter bins. Planting of trees and shrubs, provision of play areas and open space should also be considered.

The council must, by its actions, set an example to local residents and shopkeepers. Care should be taken to see that these amenities are not only provided, but that they are in keeping with the character of the surrounding neighbourhood. Choosing a sympathetic type of street lighting in terms of the design of the standard and colour of the light emitted is a case in point.

In many towns the division of responsibility between various departments can hinder effective action for conservation. It can result in, perhaps the Highways Department, with no architectural advice, retaining responsibility for street furniture or road-widening schemes, whilst the Planning Department is responsible for the Conservation Policy. A Joint Committee at both officer and councillor levels would be a useful innovation in any town but especially in a town with a Conservation Area.

Councils should seek close co-operation with statutory undertakings to ensure that unsightly overhead wires and the numerous little boxes, which most streets seem to collect, are sited sympathetically. Conservation Areas may coincide with Areas of Special Advertisement Control and in defining a Conservation Area the council should decide if such a designation should be sought. It should, however, be remembered that many places, denuded of their advertising, become visually less lively and may in the end suffer financially (see section on tidying up, page 219).

IV. DESIGN

It has previously been suggested that a Conservation Policy must aim to preserve what is valuable from the past and discipline or inspire what must change.

The identification of what we desire to preserve is relatively straightforward, despite individual tastes. The decision to preserve a building or not (the need for conversion or improvement apart) can be relatively clear cut. You cannot half preserve a building nor half knock it down, although its surrounding environment might be altered. The identification of the visual qualities that will determine townscape and architectural design disciplines is more difficult and more subjective. Design disciplines can never be so black or white, they can only influence the quality of change to ensure that new development is sympathetic in siting and design to what is preserved.

The diagram below sets out a programme of design disciplines and hypotheses which run parallel to preservation policies and make up a total conservation policy. We are now concerned with change—how and where it takes place, how it is to maintain a town's identity yet architecturally remain true to itself, how it is to be disciplined to create a sympathetic relationship with existing buildings yet avoid imitating the past.

These disciplines will affect three levels of planning. First, within the regional framework, the capabilities of the town in terms of function and size will be affected by the restrictions inherent in the design disciplines. Secondly, at town level, the planning team must be influenced by the existing

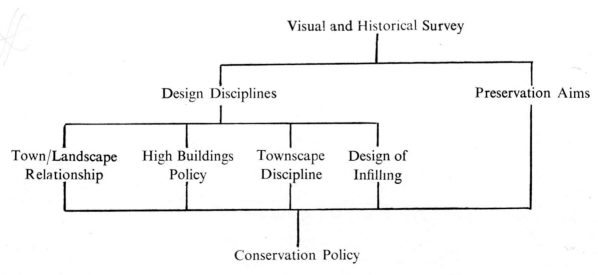

Visual and Historical Survey

Design Disciplines   Preservation Aims

Town/Landscape   High Buildings   Townscape   Design of
Relationship   Policy   Discipline   Infilling

Conservation Policy

73

form and layout of the town as a whole; its individual parts or areas of recognisable identity, and must be guided by these qualities in maintaining the town's total character. Thirdly, at the stage of development control, infilling development must be influenced by the characteristics of existing groups of buildings. These disciplines work alongside and as part of the process of policy-making; alongside the preparation of traffic proposals and economic policy, and will also, in part, be developed into public statements of policy where informed support and co-operation is required from property owners and developers. The public will need to know the local authority's basic design requirements before planning applications are made.

Design disciplines will be both protective and creative, always remaining alive to the possibility of creating new visual qualities and relationships, or emphasising existing ones and creating new feelings of local identity where none exist already. There will be four main aspects of design to be covered:

Town/Landscape Relationship—The appearance of the town as seen in the setting of the countryside.

High Buildings—The skylines and focal points.

Townscape Discipline—The qualities of space and layout which create a local discipline.

Design of Infilling—The architectural effect of new buildings inserted in existing streets.

The diagram, page 73, shows the relationship of these design disciplines.

The aspects of design described will affect both the work done by the planning team, and the public, through public relations, although the divisions are never hard and fast. In general the town/landscape relationship and townscape discipline will mainly affect work on the planning team. The aims for high buildings will concern both the planning team and be part of a public relations exercise. The design of infilling will be essentially a matter for public education.

Town/Landscape Relationship

We have already said that the size of a town, that is the number of people who live there, is fundamental to its identity. Its size is never more apparent than when the town is seen as a collection of buildings in relation to the surrounding countryside. In a village or small town the countryside is always present. In some villages the buildings are incidental to the landscape. In others the buildings huddle together, keeping out the landscape but still reminding us of its presence by giving occasional glimpses of countryside between the buildings. Particular features like well-defined boundaries and landscape features such as streams, valleys and woods must be noted.

The larger the settlement the less the presence of countryside is felt. But whatever the size of the town this relationship is still important to its identity. A distinct individual character in the change from town to countryside is essential if a town is to be a recognisable and separate entity.

The visual aims of a landscape policy must of course be tested against land availability, capacity for drainage and traffic generation as well as agricultural requirements. It is particularly important that landscape policies are backed by sound economics. The retention or adaptation of land in units which encourage efficient farming is an essential background to decisions on town boundaries. Small parcels of arable or grazing land, left isolated by development on one side and perhaps woodland on the

In a village or small town, the landscape is always present.

75

other, will not be an economic proposition. If development is halted to create the maximum visual effect, the unit of land outside the urban fence or boundary line must itself be large enough to farm or to have access from adjacent farm land. Similarly if woodland is to be preserved it may need to be a large enough area to crop.

There is always the problem of vandalism on land that immediately surrounds a built-up area. Damage to fences and crops, and the dumping of rubbish are a nuisance to farmers, and a local authority may find that in order to retain this land as an open space and permanently fix a boundary, it may need to purchase the land and maintain it as public open space.

Much damage can be avoided by planning the boundaries of a town to provide public open space as a buffer between farm or woodland. Facilities can be offered for such pastimes as riding and walking. This type of open space, freely available to the public, is a useful addition to the provision of more formal recreational spaces or sports grounds and is likely to become more important in the future.

For years good landscape has been recognised as a valuable amenity and has been protected with varying degrees of obligation and success. Green Belts, Areas of Outstanding Natural Beauty and Areas of High Landscape Value have been defined. These are chosen principally for their inherent quality of landscape or unique pattern of vegetation. The Green Belts are also chosen mainly because of their close proximity to urban development.

Now a further consideration must also be taken into account in deciding which land should be built on and which should not. The visual relationship between town and country must create a distinct visual identity for the town. Many towns already have that relationship and it ought to be maintained and enhanced. Others, through aimless development over a number of years, have lost any identifiable or meaningful boundary. A careful assessment of topography and landscape can suggest where development might take place to advantage and where it should stop in order to create a new striking boundary.

This is not to say that every town must have a hard edge that baldly states where the town ends and the countryside begins. Some towns owe their character to the way in which their edges blend with the landscape so that the change from one to the other is gradual and almost imperceptible.

These differences from one town to another are just the qualities of identity that ought to be maintained, or, where they have been lost, re-created. The first job will be to establish the nature of the underlying land form of the town and the surrounding countryside, going on to find out what the relationship of town to landscape is at present and what the historical and geographical reasons for the siting of the town and its boundaries were and the archaeological value and visual effects of those factors today.

76

Of all the strands of design policy the implementation of a Town/Landscape policy ought to present the least difficulty—providing of course there are regional and county growth patterns which have taken conservation into account. The Urban Structure Map or Local Plan will show the extent and direction of development that is desired. It will show among other things areas for development, proposed recreational open space, and limits of wedges of countryside at the town boundaries. A County Map will define areas of Special Landscape Value and Recreational Policies.

In towns of under 50,000 population it is proposed that the Minister of Housing and Local Government should have the power to require or accept submission of urban plans—for example historic towns of national importance or areas which are planned for major expansion. This might be taken to include the landscape setting of those towns.

Town/Landscape Relationship—the Town as a Whole

The town/landscape relationship is concerned with the appearance of the town in its countryside setting. The widest level of a town's identity is its overall form and its relationship to the landscape. It is important that this relationship should be definite and recognisable. In the countryside around almost every town there are a number of vantage points from which views can be obtained, giving an immediate impression of the town's shape and size. Each town will be different. When views are taken from approach roads, a bypass, a railway or from country walks, a single town may develop several different relationships to the landscape.

Bath, above, owes much of its character to its landscape setting and the views out to surrounding countryside.

Some towns, top of facing page, because they are sited on higher ground stand out in contrast to the surrounding landscape. Their larger buildings might emphasise this contrast. Others, centre, merge with the landscape and seem to lie flat upon it. Bottom: this town is tucked away between surrounding hills. The woods hide it until you have almost reached its boundaries.

As you approach a town its relationship to the countryside may change. From a distance, the town is first seen between the hills over to the right.

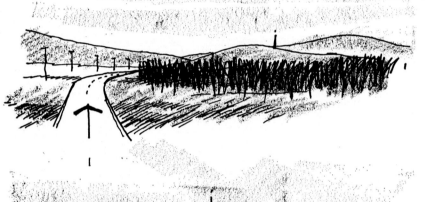

Now, as you come round the bend, it has disappeared. . .

. . . only to appear again straight ahead.

The approach has been continually ahead, but the impressions of the town have differed. If new development were allowed to spread out undisciplined by the qualities of surrounding landscape, below, it would smudge the town's identity.

Boundaries

Perhaps the most striking and obvious boundary is the natural one of the sea shore. Because the boundary is so sharp, there is always a clear distinction between the feeling between being in the town and protected by its buildings, and that of being outside the town on the beach. At Brighton, above, the hard urban fence is one of the town's main sources of character.

Not all towns can achieve such a contrast and it would be very dull if all did. Variety is essential to individual character. Where a town's boundary is indefinite, below, and development dribbles off imperceptibly into countryside, this may be an essential part of its character. Even an outer ring road or new buildings may harden up a boundary that should remain soft, bottom drawing.

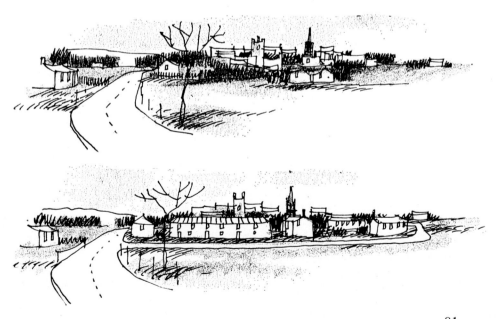

In deciding where boundaries between town and countryside will create the best visual relationship, it will be found that the shape of natural features such as hills, valleys or woods will give clues to the siting of new development. One of the principal aims ought to be the retention of the form of the land as a recognisable unit, for example a hill or a valley which create a definite boundary.

Left: development occupies the valley below, leaving clear the slopes on each side.

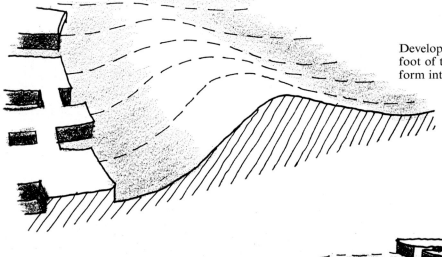

Development stops short at the foot of the hill, leaving the land form intact.

Development stops over the ridge, keeping both sides of the valley open

Around some towns there is no obvious point where development ought to stop. But where there is a natural boundary it should be used. The landscape will indicate where to call a halt and where there might be an opportunity for new development. Here a line of trees suggests a boundary.

In Haworth the buildings cluster round the hill top and the church. There is a firm boundary between the village and the countryside, but the sheds begin to blur this boundary.

The shape of Polperro, left, is disciplined by the surrounding land form; a steep-sided valley winds back from the sea and development follows the same shape. The distinct land form should continue to influence the siting of new development if the town's character is to be maintained. Below left: a discipline for new development. Below right: the discipline ignored.

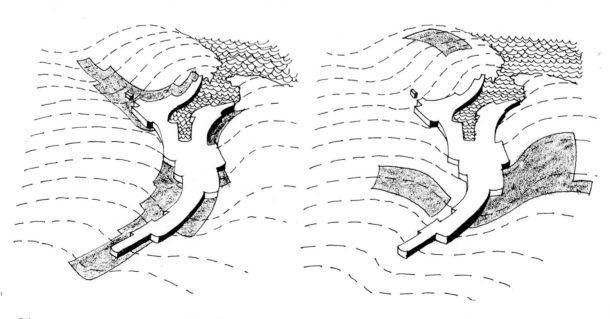

In Stamford, above, the flood plain of the river Welland penetrates the centre of the town, dividing it and bringing in the countryside. Where buildings once stood (compare map with photograph), a car park now blurs the boundary.

There might be an opportunity to put back the buildings, above, keeping the car park but maintaining the sharp distinction between town and countryside.

In Stamford again, the approach from the south shows, above, how a bend in the road and adjacent trees create a sharp distinction between town and country. The view down St. Martin's is hidden and is all the more impressive when it eventually comes into view, top of facing page. See plan below for viewpoints. However well meaning a tree-planting scheme may be, the planting of trees in St. Martin's, bottom of facing page, would destroy the contrast between being inside and being outside the town. The boundary of the town would be much less decisive.

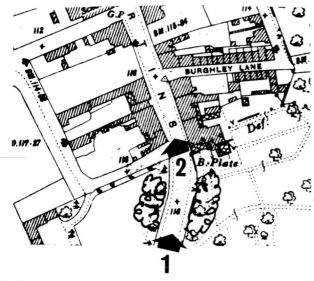

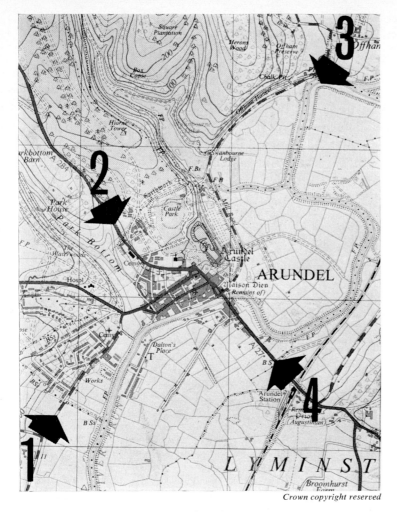

The approach roads to Arundel, see map, each offer different views of the town because of its relationship to the landscape. The town is situated on south-facing slopes above a level plain, left. This has created a special character for the town and a variety of settings for its two principal buildings, the church and the castle. In looking for areas where new development could take place, the principal views into the town centre should be protected. The three sketches, opposite and overleaf, show development allowed to spread out over the surrounding countryside and the effect this would have upon the views in the photographs, destroying the setting of the church and castle and the recognisable relationship of the town to the landscape.

View 1: from the south-west the land is flat and the town on the high ground is seen in contrast to the landscape. The church dominates the view and the castle is almost out of sight

View 2: from the
north-west the town
is hidden by the lie
of the land and the
adjoining woods. The
first sign of the
town's presence is
the sudden and dra-
matic appearance of
the church on a bend
on the road.

View 3: from the
north-east the town
is completely hidden
from view by a tree-
covered ridge of
land; only the castle
can be seen.

View 4: the south-east approach is straight across an open plain. The town's edge is well-defined: the castle rises on one side of the road, the church on the other.

Views Out

Just as important as the views of a town from the outside are those outwards from inside the town which suggest its relationship to surrounding countryside. They will also give an impression of the town's size. In Richmond, Yorkshire, there is a panoramic view across the river valley on the eastern boundary of the town, see facing page. The dribble of development, visible at the top of the photograph, is just enough to destroy the difference between town and country.

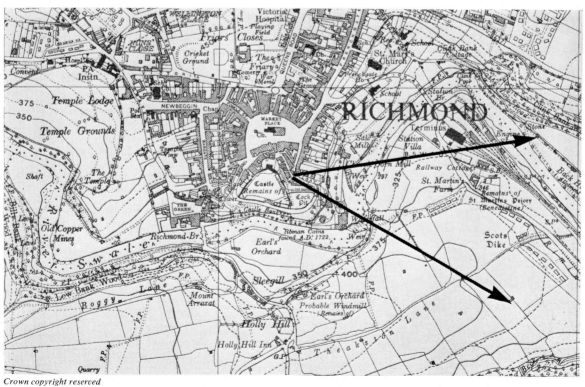

91

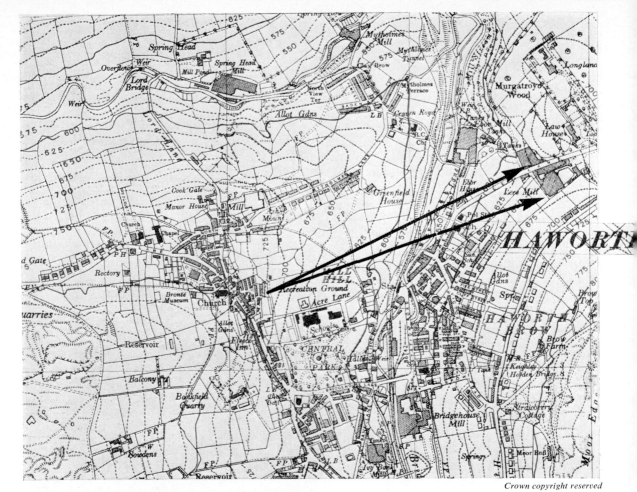

In Haworth the view out between the houses links the village to the countryside and the nearby mills, above and facing page. The contrast between inside and outside is emphasised by the narrowness of the gap between the walls.

In Portsmouth, left, the contrast is even more dramatic. The view out from behind the sea wall at Point Battery is through a narrow passage, exaggerating the difference between urban enclosure and the open Solent. It is therefore not only what is seen in the view that is important, but it is also the way in which it is seen that creates a special sense of locality.

The combination of different types of view out and the discipline of their arrangement can be a strong factor in creating local character. Lewes High Street, above, on high ground just below the castle, has two different types of view out—a broad panoramic view east at the end of the street and many small tightly enclosed views, photogaphs on facing page, down the lanes to the south. This contrast of viewpoints plays a big part in giving the street a particular character.

Change the arrangement and you change the character. Upper plan, facing page: new development opening up panoramic views to the south would alter the contrast of views and would destroy the enclosure and rhythm of the street; lower plan: it might still be possible to provide a pedestrian square which would maintain the enclosure of the street and incorporate another narrow view to the south.

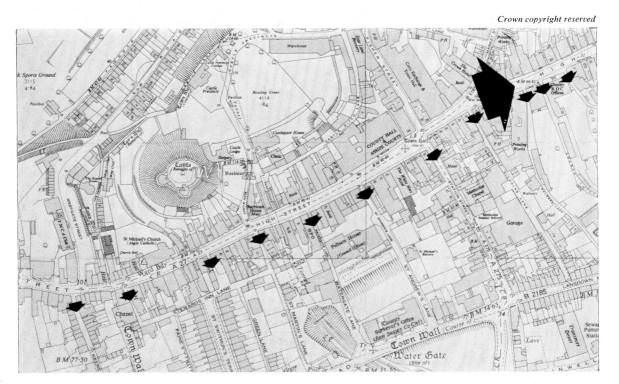

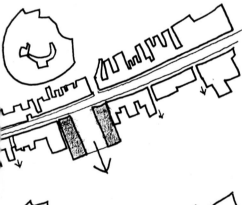

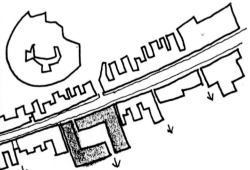

High Buildings

A High Buildings Policy works at two main levels. Firstly it will set out a number of principles for the siting of large or tall buildings with the aim of maintaining or emphasising existing town skylines and sometimes creating positive new ones. Secondly it will safeguard local views within the town, where either the scale or the skyline warrant protection. The policy may be directed towards maintaining the setting of a group of historic buildings.

It is necessary to define exactly what a tall building is. A tall building in a small market town might only be regarded as a small building in a large city. So the scale or general height of existing development is what determines whether or not a proposed building is high, and whether it ought to be considered visually over a wider area than its immediate site.

The underlying land form will dramatically affect the way in which high buildings are seen and may suggest opportunities for making or emphasising new development.

It is not only the height of a building that matters, but it is often its bulk and outline as well. In a city, where the height and spiky outline of a cathedral is the focus of interest over the whole town, new buildings must maintain the dominance of the cathedral and respect the skyline.

Most small towns are still dominated by the spire of a church, and many large towns have perhaps one or two central spires and several smaller churches which mark out the centres of residential areas. These act almost as signposts for parts of the town, and their combination into a visual whole may well be the largest single factor in determining the identity and legibility of the town when seen from the outside. This does not necessarily imply that new development could not create such an effect, but it is unlikely to improve upon the spires and towers of churches and a total ban on new high buildings may be necessary.

The purpose and function of towns change. The significance of a church spire for a town and its surrounding countryside is different now from its original inspirational one. In many towns today, a tall office building might have more significance. The flour mills at Selby probably have that significance for the town now. The cooling towers of a power station can provide just as powerful a signpost for a town (if not quite as decorative) as the church spire has in the past. These towers are often extremely helpful in providing orientation points in the suburbs, for example. The real problem centres around the contrast and conflict between these new forms and the old. The bulk of the new and the fine spiky quality of the old seldom go well together.

For economic reasons offices and flats are usually built long and fat

High Buildings: the Town as a Whole

In drawing up a policy for high buildings one of the first things to examine will be the views of the town as a whole as seen from the outside. In many towns there will be no opportunity for erecting high buildings. Salisbury, for example, is dominated by its cathedral spire from views of the city on many of its approaches and in the surrounding countryside. New high buildings, left, are probably unacceptable over the whole city area: though not necessarily masking the spire of the Cathedral, they would change the identity of the town.

rather than tall and slim. In small domestic-scale towns this is a great disadvantage. Tall thin buildings can more easily be designed to sit side by side with the delicate church spires than the long fat ones.

A High Buildings Policy which decides to preserve the existing general building height and the dominance of a number of churches above that height may well need to be accompanied by proposals for changes of use for the churches, if they are under-used. The new uses which are found would need to be compatible with the importance of the building in the town. For example, they might form a focal point for part of the civic centre or public library or art gallery. Similarly, where new buildings are to dominate the skyline they should, wherever possible, represent local civic interests: not the interests of one commercial firm competing with another. The Buckinghamshire County Hall at Aylesbury is a good example of a high building focusing attention on a civic function. (See illustration page 103.)

The detailed design of tall buildings is as critical as their siting, if only because of being tall they are seen from many more viewpoints. Again, the Aylesbury building is well modelled and is, consequently, more visually interesting than the usual glass box which, being flat and bulky, is more difficult to assimilate.

In smaller towns the breaking up and modelling of large surfaces on tall buildings, indicating the room sizes and floor heights, gives a sense of human scale which can be related to the domestic scale of the town around it. In a large metropolitan city the scale of townscape is more overpowering and it can assimilate more massive units. This is one of the qualities which gives the centre of a conurbation or very large city a different identity from the centre of a small town.

The need for tall residential blocks is likely to be confined for the most part to the larger towns and cities where land is at a premium and there is a vigorous slum clearance programme.

Office and residential development offer opportunities to create points of interest in the endless suburban sprawl which surrounds so many large cities, new tall buildings can mark out district centres, and residential blocks bring life and vitality at night to otherwise dead shopping centres. One incidental quality of tall residential buildings is their effect at night, acting as giant illuminated signposts that can be seen for miles around.

Like other broad design policies the siting of high buildings must be assessed in conjunction with wider aspects of planning. The visual aims must be tested for feasibility and compatibility with other planning aims. For example, high buildings bringing greater concentrations of office workers or residents, must be especially examined for their effect on traffic generation.

When design aims have been tested at an early stage and when their effect

98

on other land use and transportation proposals is assessed before they are finalised, the resultant policy, though perhaps modified, will have a good chance of success.

The implementation of a High Buildings Policy often requires a strong public relations effort. It must nevertheless be backed by a regional or sub-regional policy for the distribution of large-scale office accommodation and must attempt to create demand where, other considerations apart, a town would benefit visually from tall buildings, while removing the pressure where the skyline is to be kept intact.

In towns where high buildings are to be accepted, the degree to which their siting can be controlled will depend firstly on publicity. It is essential that developers who wish to make planning applications should be warned of the authorities' intentions and objectives. Redevelopment in areas where tall buildings are not desirable can be restricted by means of an established plot ratio accompanied by height restrictions on buildings. The Group Design Discipline for Infilling, described later in this book, should also assist in creating a climate of opinion which will aid the control of development and be a useful adjunct to plot ratio technique. However, these restrictions must be backed by good public relations which emphasise, not just the restrictions, but also the opportunities on alternative sites.

In Lichfield, new blocks of flats conflict with the cathedral spires—there is no longer a simple, strong character.

The skyline of Ludlow, top of facing page, is instantly recognizable from the south: another example of a town where new high buildings should be prohibited.
Bottom of facing page, in Burford, for example, or in parts of towns such as conservation areas, high buildings ought to be prohibited completely, either because there is a large collection of historic buildings or because the overall scale and size should remain domestic.

New buildings do not necessarily have to be tall to spoil the whole character of a town. In Guildford this department store overpowers the domestic scale; a more broken outline would have helped.

New buildings can sometimes be used, below, to add to the character of a town which has no existing tall buildings.

While many reasons can be given for restricting
high buildings, there are plenty of places where
they can be a positive advantage and they can be
used to create a new visual effect. We can learn
from the past: Salisbury or Durham cathedrals
are important because they express something of
the activity and function of those cities, and so
have a local significance. New high buildings ought
also to have some significance for the local community. They should not be there as a status symbol
for a firm or an architect. In Aylesbury the new
County Council building has great significance for
the town and the surrounding countryside.

Views Across the Town

Certain local views of significant buildings are important to a town's character and set up relationships between different areas. They express the structure and visual organisation of the town. In Stamford, a strong visual link exists between an outlying residential area and the town centre.

continued opposite

In Bath, left, the reverse occurs. From the centre there is a long distance view out to a church tower in a residential area. New high buildings in the wrong place, drawing below, could shut out this view.

continued

A distant view across the river valley, top of facing page, links the houses to one of the church towers in the town centre. Ill-sited large scale development, bottom left on facing page, could destroy this relationship. In a few instances, though not in Stamford, new offices in the town centre might replace a church tower, bottom right of facing page, and perform the same visual function as the original tower.

In Torquay, the main shopping street
is in a steep-sided valley. The combination of land form and buildings creates
a striking character which could be
destroyed by high level development
in the wrong place. Tall buildings in
the high street, left, would also obstruct
views from one side of the valley to
the other.

In Nottingham there is a central park high up on the castle mount from which there used to be views across to the dome of the city hall and the higher buildings in the central area: New buildings on Maid Marion Way now obliterate the views from this important city park.

Focal Points

In the City of London the Guildhall, below right, is the centre of the whole of the City's activities. But a new office block, sited immediately behind the Guildhall, below left, confuses the image and lessens the impact of the buildings. There are plenty of opportunities for tall buildings in the City and sometimes a contrast of scale can emphasise the impact of the focal point.

In Selby, Yorkshire, the Abbey is the focal point of the long slow-curving High Street. As one moves along the street the Abbey emerges as the most important building. An intrusive building on the curve of the High Street, shown below left, would create an unwanted intermediate focal point and distract attention from the main point of interest.

In Stamford High Street, right, St. Michael's church tower provides an indirect focal point: it is no longer the dominating feature of the street, but is seen over the street façade.

In many areas a series of focal points combine together to create a strong image over a large area or along a street. Three buildings in High Street, Chapel Street and Church Street, Stratford upon Avon provide a series of focal points in succession. First the Town Hall, then the Guild Chapel, then finally an eighteenth century house, each dominate a section of the street, one giving way to the next. The visual combination of focal points helps to hold the street together as a visual entity. Assuming that the buildings are to be preserved, new buildings ought to respect this delicate rhythm. The new tall building sketched in on the photograph below, interrupts and breaks the rhythm.

Sometimes one building acts as a focal point for
a whole street. In Warwick the church tower creates
a formal visual stop to the street: new tall buildings,
head of facing page, obviously should not disturb
the formality of this view.

A building that is tall in a small town, below left, might be regarded as insignificant in a large town, below right.

A town with an existing and valuable focal point on a flat plain, may present little opportunity for high buildings.

New high buildings invariably conflict with the existing focal point whether they are in front,

or behind,

or to one side.

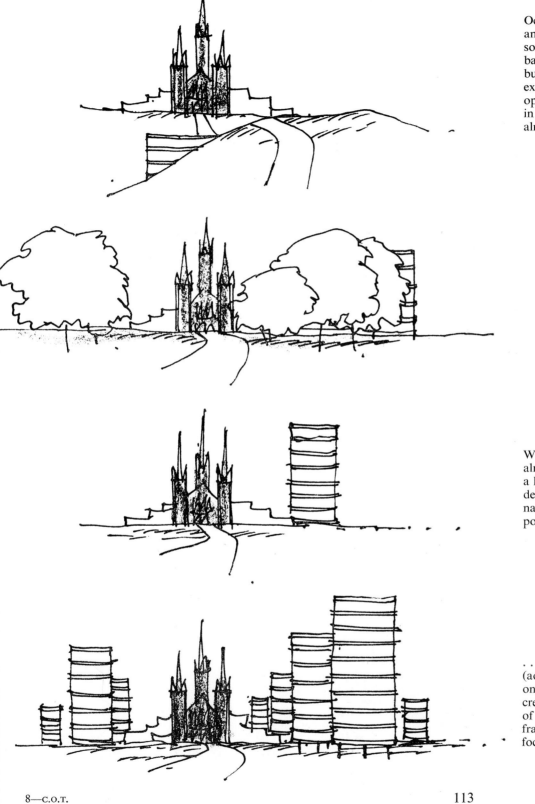

Occasionally the rise and fall of land, or some other visual barrier, trees or buildings for example, creates the opportunity to slip in a high building almost unnoticed.

Where a mistake has already occurred and a high building has destroyed the dominance of the focal point . . .

. . . the only solution (admittedly a bold one) might be to create a whole series of new buildings to frame the original focal point.

Opportunity

Facing page: occasionally a park or open space in a town has a rural quality which, though imaginary, ought to be protected. On the other hand, an open space with no particular character may be made more attractive as a frankly urban park with high buildings placed around it, bottom of facing page, where here is an opportunity for flats.

This page, above: opportunities will also occur for high buildings where new roads carry fast-moving traffic. The massing and scale of buildings can be better appreciated if it is geared to the speed of the onlooker's movement.

In a town with a central square that has become drab and uninteresting or is really too wide and open to have any visual impact, a tall building might give new significance to the square, left.

115

The office development in Croydon (there are not many pleasant views of it) demonstrates the importance of the borough as a commercial centre in South London, above.

While it is essential to maintain the scale and privacy of the residential areas, this office block in Gants Hill is a welcome visual relief to endless suburban boredom, below.

In an existing street (particularly in a big city) an opportunity may occur to insert a high building by setting it back on a lower podium. The podium maintains the normal street façade and the high building rises relatively harmlessly behind. New Zealand House, in London, is a good example of this (at least in this view).

In St. James's Street, London, the tower of the new Economist building being set back in its own courtyard and behind a small block of street-façade height, does not disrupt the scale of the area.

117

Townscape Discipline

The economic, geographical and political forces that have caused towns to be established have resulted in many different forms of town. Towns built on a crossroads or with a wall around them; towns that have clustered round a castle, cathedral close or a market place; towns with a waterfront; towns on a river; holiday towns, towns based on industry; all have a different impact and are often of intrinsic archaeological interest.

Furthermore, towns grew up on different landscapes and on different land forms, each one drawing from the landscape part of its identity. On these different sites were constructed an infinite variety of buildings, so that no two towns are alike.

Our towns have nearly all expanded haphazardly and have been renewed in a piecemeal way over many years. The spaces between buildings have taken on quite unique characteristics in each town because of this piecemeal growth.

Here, though accidentally obtained, is a powerful source of local identity. This piecemeal quality is not only easily recognisable and often picturesque, but also creates townscape which has vitality and compactness and in many cases is unique enough to be of international historic interest.

These are the qualities, which at this particular time, are most threatened. They cannot be saved simply by keeping a few historic buildings, because in many cases the majority of the buildings which create these qualities are not historic or worth preserving in themselves. We now need a special design approach which is co-ordinated and disciplined by the overall quality of the townscape.

Not only does the increased use of vehicles of all sorts challenge the validity of urban compactness and compactness of population, but it also threatens the form and layout of towns. The gridiron layouts and the meandering streets, the city walls and gates of old towns are obstacles to free movement. In the same way, development of all sorts—shops, offices, roads and car parks—challenges the spatial organisation of our towns and their domestic scale.

It has been said that conservation is a double-edged policy; it must preserve what is valuable and influence what must change. Much of the townscape can be preserved if the pressures for change can be diverted. Where it must change in response to those pressures it should be rebuilt within the discipline of a local identity, not reproducing the same thing again but interpreting specific local qualities and learning from them, in order to continue what has been called "the grain of the place".

This is not to say that new development and solutions to contemporary

118

problems of road provision and car parking cannot create satisfactory new forms within an old environment. However, the fact that they seldom do, cannot be ignored. They need a local discipline.

There is another reason for accepting the discipline of the existing townscape. Archaeological features such as town walls or road layout cannot be left as isolated shapes on the map in totally unrelated new development. If they are to be preserved they must be given both a physical and visual meaning as part of the contemporary urban fabric; new and old combining to create a sense of unity.

In order to achieve this sense of unity these older forms must to some degree influence the visual design of new development; the siting of roads, the relationship of new spaces to existing spaces and of new massing to old massing.

Local authorities will probably have to relax certain planning standards if compactness is to be maintained. Provisions concerning verges, street widths, pavement widths, sight lines and daylighting angles may need to be modified substantially (for example to avoid these minor improvements the capacity of an area to carry traffic without such changes must be assessed and traffic flows in excess of that capacity diverted).

The townscape is of course, not just a matter of bricks and mortar; it is also concerned with atmosphere and personal experience. The architect on the planning team must get the feel of the townscape and communicate that experience to his colleagues. This is the least objective part of the architect's work but certain aspects of townscape are fundamental and usually occur quite frequently and therefore can be quite easily recognised. It is the exceptions, however, which must be watched for most carefully. They are the qualities which create individuality.

The architect must work to a check list of jobs to be done, and his appraisal of survey material and the conclusions that are drawn up from that survey must be presented in a way that is clear and precise. A few sketches and photographs of the best parts of the town are no substitute for a well-documented and mapped survey. The traffic engineer, the estates surveyor and the land-use planner on the team will want evidence as well as inspiration from the appraisal if they are to be convinced of the value of and influenced by the aesthetic conclusions.

The architect must record his impression of a town; the way its spaces are organised and enclosed, the unities of scale and place within the overall fabric, and the visual relationships of one part to another. He must show the cracks between one part and another where opportunites for change exist. He must point out the opportunities for creating new townscape.

Some parts of the survey and appraisal, such as those dealing with enclosure of space as it affects individual sites, could usefully be publicised in the same document as that on the design of infilling.

119

Opportunity

The discipline inherent in the town-scape can be the source of new ideas and opportunities, both in redevelopment and in the renewal and improvement of existing areas. Improvements can begin at the simplest and cheapest level, as in this example at Gentleman's Row, Enfield, where a riverside walk has been improved by the removal of old fencing.

In Reading, Castle Street is a main traffic route west from the town centre. There are just enough buildings of quality for something new to be built around them. There might be a chance to remove through traffic and build an enclave next to the centre for houses and offices, with local traffic only—a new environment and lease of life for the older buildings. Someone may even put the cupola back.

With an eye to see the possibilities inherent in a
town, this church, St. Mary's Butts, in Reading,
could become the focal point of a new square, away
from the traffic, facing page, and enclosed by
houses or small offices. Close to the town centre,
it would provide a quiet retreat for a rest from the
bustle of shopping.

So many towns have areas that have been forgotten. Natural features often seem to deteriorate into sad dreary places, and rivers seem to suffer more than most. In this part of Reading, cars take over the last inch (and more) of tow-path, where people should be walking and enjoying the waterside. Let the industry and offices stay, they give the place an individual identity, but also realise the natural potential as a place for people, drawing below.

In Knaresborough, Yorkshire, an opportunity has been taken and the riverside is well used for recreation.

126

Facing page: a scattered collection of rather poor eighteenth-century cottages offers an opportunity to create a stronger group of buildings by adding more houses in the gaps, perhaps a local shop, below left. This would give a sense of roots for a small new estate, and a longer life for the existing cottages.

Stamford, Lincolnshire, this page, remains largely unscathed. But here are two places where opportunity exists to improve the townscape.

The east end of St. George's Square, above, has lost its sense of enclosure and the garage does not do much for the square's architectural quality. Re-siting the garage and erecting new houses would increase the sense of enclosure and the space would regain its integrity.

127

Another Stamford opportunity on the most prominent site in the town. The approach into the town centre from the south culminates in a view of backyards, above. There is already a little formal scheme, incomplete since the 18th century. There may be an opportunity here to complete the scheme and create a better climax for the way in.

128

Often the mere age of one or two buildings makes them an important feature of a wider group of buildings. In Malt Mill Lane, Alcester, a group of cottages have been put on the Statutory List of Historic Buildings for their group value. They are of no intrinsic architectural value in themselves and the only reason for listing them is that their scale, use of materials and age seem important to the street as a whole. It might however be argued that a new building in the street could help maintain the commercial value of the existing buildings by arousing interest in the street as a pleasant place in which to live. Opportunity taken in the right place can have far-reaching economic effects over a large area.

Townscape Discipline: Identity Areas

The townscape discipline is concerned with the shape
of the town—discovering what exists now and
learning how this might influence new development
so that it maintains continuity. In some cases the
shape of the town or parts of it might be preserved.
One of the first jobs in drawing up a townscape
discipline is to define areas with a complete identity.
In small settlements the whole built-up area might
be considered as having an overall identity. In larger
towns certain areas will stand out as having different
visual and social identities. Where conservation is
concerned the aim ought.to be the retention of each
area as an entity.

One of the objects in defining these areas of visual
identity may be to suggest environmental areas.
The shape of a conservation area might be suggested
by one or more identity areas, see page 51. By
defining such areas over a town as a whole, their
boundaries or the marginal areas of land between
them, will suggest possible lines for new road net-
works or the siting of other developments such as
car parks.

The town as a whole, or in a large city the city
centre, may be divided into a number of major
identity areas, perhaps determined by their overall
scale or use, the land form or the city walls.
With these major areas local identity areas, determined more by street pattern, enclosed or open
spaces or other visual entities, will be bound to
exist.   The diagram, right, shows a typical arrangement of local identity areas in the centre of a small
town (the survey drawing on page 239 illustrates
another example on a base map). Each area is given
a lettered grade to indicate its relative importance
to conservation. A diagrammatic conservation area
is indicated by the pecked line. An urban crack
appears between certain areas and is shown by the
solid line, suggesting a possible alignment for a
local distributor road.

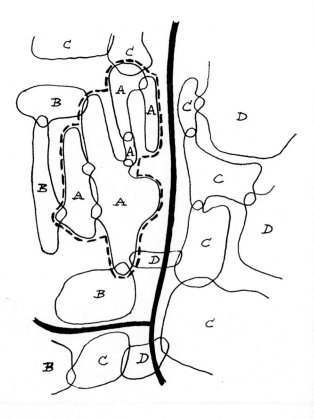

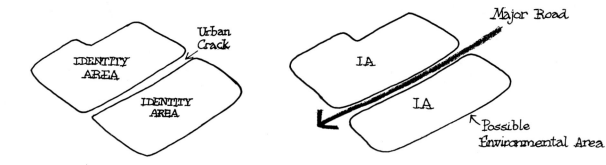

The crack between two adjoining areas may well suggest the line of a new major traffic route.

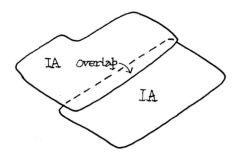

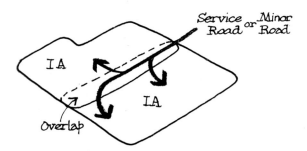

Where identity areas overlap, that is where it is difficult to distinguish between them and where there may be strong pedestrian communication, it may be necessary to treat the two as one, not allowing the intrusion of any major road, at most that of a minor or service road.

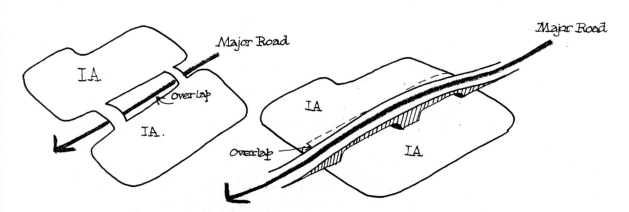

Where a major network is unavoidable between two overlapping areas it may need to be sunk below the surface or raised above it to allow free pedestrian movement. Where there is a strong visual connection between two areas to sink the road might be the better solution. More usually, overlapping identity areas might suggest the line of a service road.

131

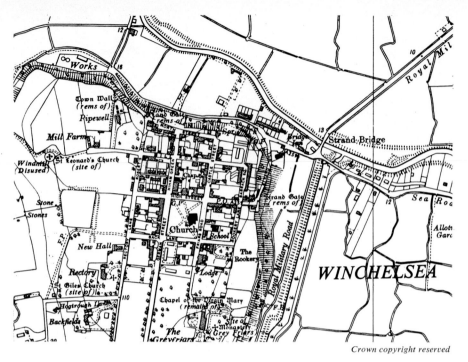

In the small town of Winchelsea, left, the gridiron road pattern determines the identity of the whole town, any small scale extension of such a town might continue the same road pattern.

In Sandwich, left, the town walls remain to mark the boundaries of the old town. These enclose a wide identity area. New high-density development (in the areas shown in black) might be contained within the town walls to avoid using up more of the surrounding countryside and to emphasise the importance of the walls and the difference between being inside and outside the historic core.

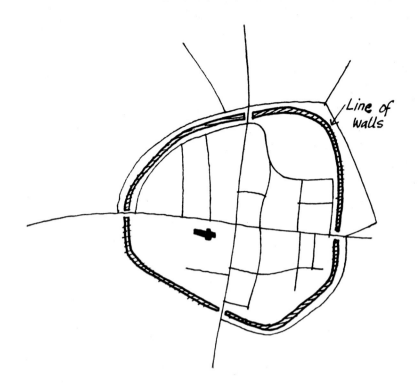

Line of
walls

In Chichester city
centre a number of
identity areas or
visual entities can be
found, but over-
riding these local
identity areas the
the central cross
shape of the roads
spanning the wide
area out to the line
of the city walls,
creates one major
identity area, upper
drawing. The pro-
posed ring road
pattern, lower
drawing, is deter-
mined by the shape
and extent of the
whole unit.

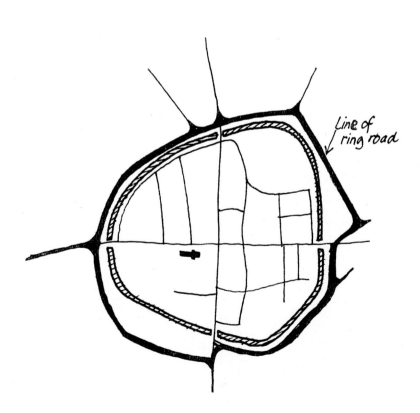

Line of
ring road

Sometimes the way in which buildings have been constructed and are organised together in relation to the landscape establishes a distinct feeling of locality over a certain area.

In New Quay, Wales, a series of terraces follows the contours of the hillside; an area of identity is established. New roads ought to respect the total identity of this area and not, for example, slice across the contour lines. Similarly, new development should respect the discipline or grain of existing buildings; it should maintain the form of building in terraces following the contours.

Below: development disturbing the local grain and destroying the visual continuity of the identity area.

In Torquay the buildings on the hill are sparse and interspersed with trees yet there is a definite visual unity to this part of the town; quite different from the adjoining shopping street (see illustration, page 106). The land form suggests an identity area.

In Liverpool, above, the central business district is held together visually by its overall scale.

A common scale of buildings often goes hand-in-hand with a common activity. In Nottingham, left, the extent of the Old Lace Market is easily recognised by its continuity of scale and similarity of architecture.

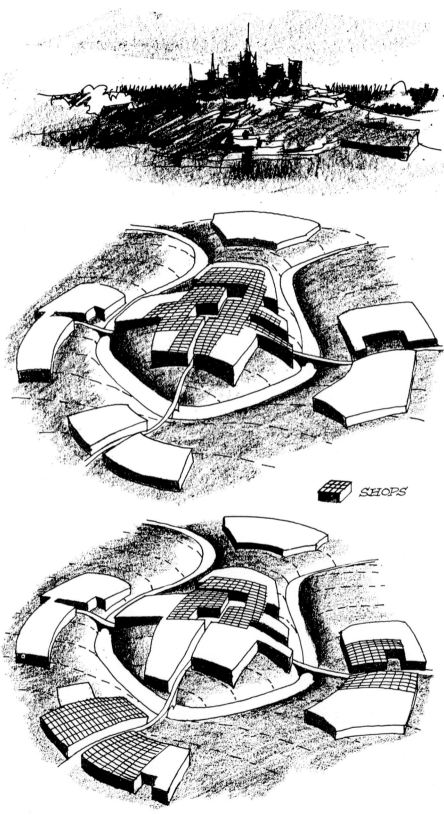

SHOPS

In many towns a clear relationship exists between individual areas of identity and activity and the underlying land form. The maintenance of this relationship is usually essential to the town's character. The centre may be on the highest ground, left, or have the highest buildings and so stand out from the residential areas. In Shrewsbury, centre and bottom drawings, and Durham, the centre is on a spur of land almost encircled by the river. There is thus a definite discipline in the town's layout and relationship to the land form, which should be maintained if character is not to be eroded. If, as in the bottom drawing, part of the town centre were made residential, and shopping areas were added to the encircling residential areas, the significance of the historic core would be lost.

137

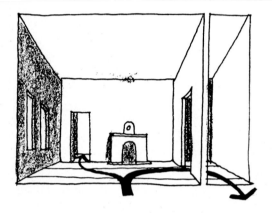

Enclosure of Space

The way in which spaces are formed between buildings is important both as a setting for the individual buildings and as a more local and detailed aspect of a town's character, in which each space takes on its own identity.

Most people are aware of the feeling of enclosure in a room. They are aware that walls, ceiling and floor form a kind of box. A space is enclosed and defined, above left, out of which, through windows and doors, one can see other rooms or the surroundings of a house. A room can be said to have its own identity.

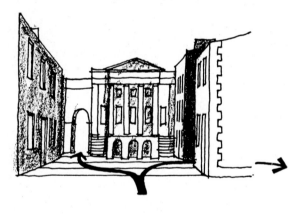

A space in a town is just the same, centre left; buildings surround the town square, enclosing space.

There are views out to other spaces. There is a floor but no ceiling, consequently the sky-line becomes most important to the sense of enclosure, bottom drawing.

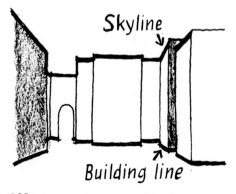

Skyline

Building line

A well-defined space becomes a small unit of identity with its own built-in design discipline, which is basically the need to maintain the enclosure.
In Liverpool a small square is situated in the centre of the city by Wyatt's town hall. There is a strong sense of enclosure despite the fact that one of the city's principal streets passes through the space.
The skyline or eaves line is strong enough to define the shape of the space.

139

In Petersfield the town's square is undergoing re-development in one corner. A building has been pulled down to make way for another. In the meantime the square is a reminder of what happens when enclosure is destroyed and the space is no longer clearly defined.

Streets are also spaces in the sense that they are enclosed by buildings. Changing building lines and skylines create different qualities of enclosure in the street.

Lewes High Street, facing page, contains different examples of the way in which a street can be effectively enclosed as a space. The enclosure, if maintained, will have a definite capacity for carrying traffic. New development ought to respect these changing building lines in order to maintain the identity of the streets.

A building projects forward to enclose a section of the street.

Looking the other way, a slight change in direction closes the view out.

Further along, the High Street is enclosed by a long curving building line.

141

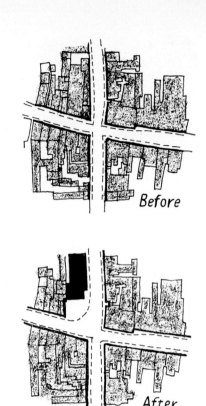

Before

After

In Stratford-upon-Avon, a new building with an ingenious (perhaps too ingenious) medieval, image is set back on a corner making a pointless space that opens up and destroys the town's firm street pattern, above. At a point which ought to be a cross roads an ill-shaped square is formed, perhaps to create better sight lines for traffic and to display the adjoining end wall: a failure to let the character of the street determine traffic capacity—an essential aspect of conservation. Before and after plans, right.

In Barnard Castle, top of facing page, the curving building line encloses the space and hides the view out of the end of the street to open countryside. The street has a long and continuous identity. In Tonbridge, bottom of facing page, the curve has been torn open, destroying the sense of enclosure and the continuity of the street.

In Newark, above, a long curving road leads up to the church. A gap in the row of buildings on the right hand side destroys the sense of enclosure creating a space without meaning. The dramatic "lead up" to the church tower is spoilt.

142

In Sandwich, New Street gets much of its identity and sense of enclosure from the gently curving building line. In this view, left, the enclosure seems complete but just past the building on the left with the bay windows, this gap, centre picture, with its garages disrupts the continuity of the building line. The enclosure is broken and the identity dissipated.

Petrol filling stations, right, are among the most difficult to absorb into the street scene. Not only are their advertisements often brash and their colour schemes crude, but they create new spaces totally unrelated to the enclosure of the street.

In Shrewsbury the street known as Wyle Cop climbs up to the town centre and has a continuous sense of enclosure due to the constantly changing building line. This adds variety to the street and is therefore important to its character (avoid widening and straightening). Continuity is maintained because the height of the buildings remains virtually the same. Notice how one façade takes over from the next in enclosing the space as one climbs the hill: the first picture, right, shows the beginning of the climb.

Character of Space

The way in which space is enclosed has already been described: each space will have its own character. The height of the buildings in relation to the width of the space enclosed determines much of that character.

In Nottingham, above and top of facing page, this street is like a corridor—the height of the buildings is greater than the width of the street.

146

Alter the height of the buildings, as in the drawing above, and the character of the space changes. It loses its identity, becoming a less successful version of this square in Richmond, below, which has a static and restful character due to its width being greater than the height of the buildings.

Sometimes a single space, such as this one in Bath, is split up by one building in the middle. The space retains its enclosure. The removal of the building would however change the character of the space.

Change of level

Change of level affects the character of different spaces. In Richmond, the market square is situated on a rising dome of land.

In Dartmouth this narrow alley-way gets its character not just from the tight enclosure, but also from the change of level. Where changes of level exist they ought to be continually exploited in new development.

Changes in level not only change the character of space but also bring an element of surprise into the townscape.

149

Activities

Local activities also give character to streets. The different functions and uses of streets will create different visual characteristics. Above: warehousing in Southwark. Facing page, top: the quayside at Whitby; bottom: street market in Soho.

150

Detailing

The residential street will obviously be different
from a shopping street. Detailing on buildings will
reflect the activities and scale of particular places.
Facing page: domestic detailing in a small town.
Above: large urban detailing in the city centre.

153

Trees

The way trees have been used in the townscape will give a clue to the identity of a place and will also help to suggest ways in which future planting may enhance local character.

There is formal planting in this square at Marl-borough, above, but the atmosphere is still that of a small rural community. Trees in Queen Square, Bath, below, and in Newbiggin, Richmond, Yorks, top of facing page, are as important to the character of the space as the buildings and the sense of enclosure.

It is just as important to recognise the places with trees and where new planting might take place as it is to recognise those without trees and where planting should not take place. This hard urban square, left, in Richmond with no trees contrasts with Newbiggin, above, a few yards away. A street with lots of activity but no trees will contrast with a quiet square filled with trees.

Contrast of Spaces

Where spaces of different character adjoin, a relationship will be set up between one space and the other. The experience of being in one space, say a tightly enclosed corridor, will contrast with the experience of being in a more open space; the one will emphasise the character and identity of the other. The two combine to create a wider area of identity. In Durham the whole area and its various parts is visually integrated into a complex organisation of spaces which together create a single identity. The views from the approach roads to the central spur of land with its enormous scale and sense of space, are masked by the buildings on either side. The enclosure of the approach road, A in sketch, contains the view until one is almost on the bridge, providing the maximum contrast between one space and the other, B.

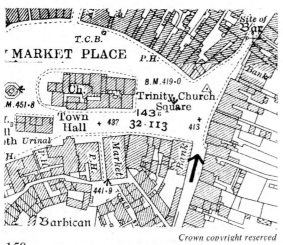

Crown copyright reserved

In Richmond, for example, there is a sharp contrast between street and square. The buildings at the end of the street and on either side frame and restrict the view out into the square and increase the contrast. One space is dependent on the next.

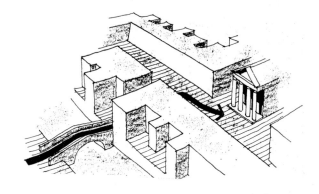

Many towns have successions of contrasting spaces. In Bridgend, South Wales, a chain of spaces, above and left, takes one across the river and into the town centre. Top photo, the crown of the bridge is open and unprotected. Beyond is a narrow space with views through to the wider street, third photo. In the tight alley, the larger space is a few steps away, and once into the street one can see into a yet larger square, dominated by the portico of the town hall, bottom left.

These interrelated contrasting spaces are a splendid approach to the building, special to Bridgend. Open up the area, and its individuality disappears, drawing below. Picture at bottom right shows changes after five years. Lighting columns are better; a traffic sign has gone. But the town hall has decayed a little more, and is now up for redevelopment, detailed changes have eroded much of the shop's interest, and the low new building has weakened the enclosure of the square.

These two pages show another series of spaces, in Stamford, leading from St. Mary's Church to St. George's Church. The sequence begins at the head of the facing page.

Organisation of Spaces

Some areas in towns stand out from others because of the character of their spaces or the layout of streets in relation to those around. Such differences between one part of the town and another suggest a spatial organisation which might well be maintained; they also suggest the boundaries of identity areas and perhaps conservation areas.

In the drawing below left, this town centre has large spaces and the surrounding residential areas have small, insignificant spaces. In the drawing below centre, the situation is reversed. In the plan below right, the centre is like a maze where the roads twist and turn and it is difficult to orientate oneself. (Look at the map of Sandwich on page 132 where the streets take on a quite distinct form from those outside.)

In Perth, left and facing page, the blocks of development form a grid-iron road pattern. New, open, ground-level car parks would destroy the character created by the existing formal development. A multi-storey car park, as shown in the small drawing, would fill a whole block so as to maintain the grid layout.

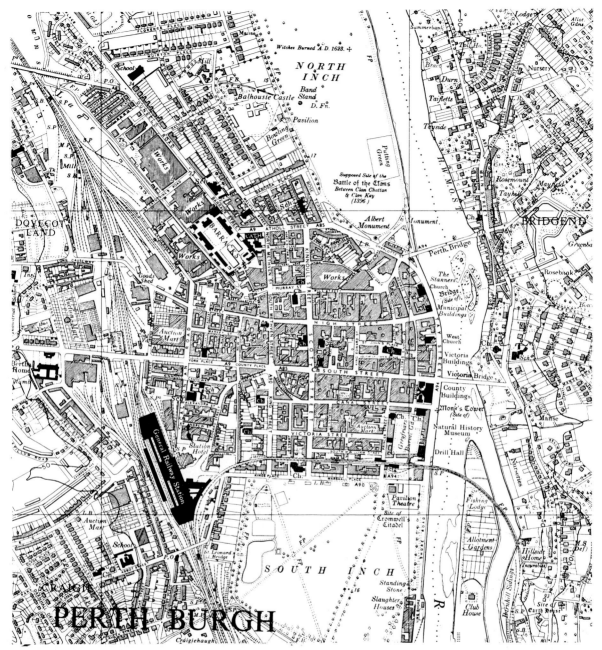

North Inch

Witches Burned A.D. 1623. +

Balhousie Castle

Band Stand
D. Fn.

Pavilion

Bowling Green

Supposed Site of the
Battle of the Clans
Between Clan Chattan
& Clan Kay
(1396)

Putting Green

DOVECOT LAND

Works

BARRACKS

CATH

Goods Shed

Works

Auction Mart

Berth Home

Albert Monument

Monument

Perth Bridge

BRIDGEND

The Stanners

Bridge
(Site of)

Municipal Buildings

West Church

Victoria Buildings

Victoria Bridge

County Buildings

Monk's Tower
(Site of)

Natural History Museum

Drill Hall

Pavilion Theatre

Site of Cromwell's Citadel

General Railway Station

Station Hotel

Auction Mart

School

St Leonard Bridge

SOUTH INCH

Standing Stone

Slaughter Houses

Fishing Lodge

Allotment Gardens

Hillside Home
Incurables

CRAIGIE

PERTH BURGH

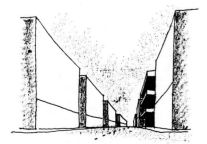

163

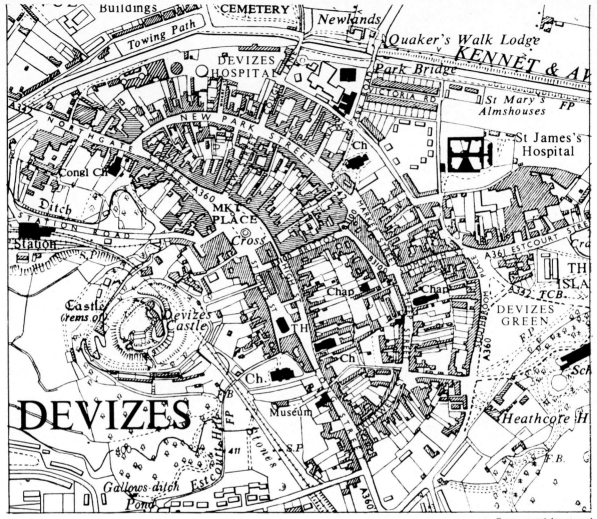

In Devizes, a long, curving road contrasts with, and encloses, an inner arrangement of spaces. If the town centre is to retain its character, new roads should be influenced by the existing pattern.

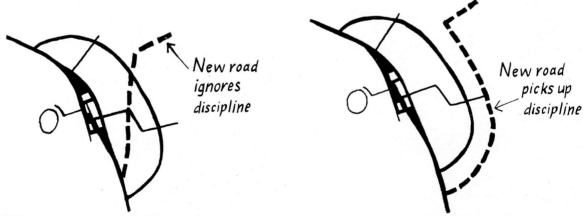

New road ignores discipline

New road picks up discipline

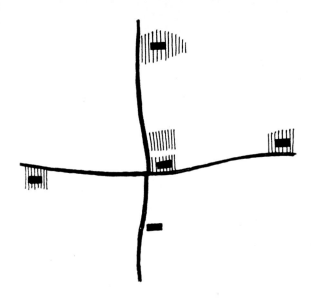

In Northampton, sketch plan left, there is a strong pattern to the town centre. From All Saints' Church and the large market square in the centre of the town, four roads lead out to the four outlying churches in residential areas. The reshaping of the central area might use this relationship as the basis for redevelopment.

In Canterbury, photograph below, new large scale spaces open the urban fabric to provide car parks. New multi-storey car parks of the right scale would be an improvement. Sites for these large open areas need to be chosen carefully to respect the existing hierarchy of spaces.

In Cirencester, bottom photograph, the same problem occurs. Despite care in detailing, the new space sits uncomfortably in the fabric of the town: again, multi-storey car parks would fill the hole.

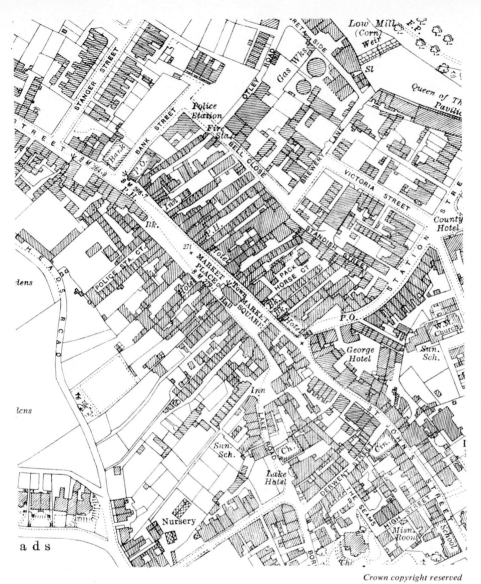

In Keswick the roads lead out from a single, central space, shown diagrammatically in drawing A, below. The plan form is essential to the town's historic character. A new car park, B, creating a larger public space than the existing market place, could destroy the spatial organisation of the town. The smaller car parks, diagram C, would be better. They are subordinate to the larger historic market place.

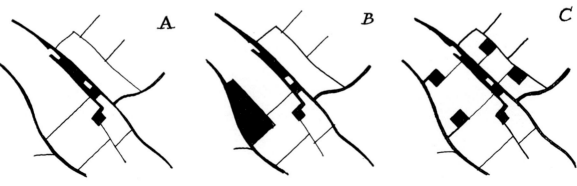

A   B   C

166

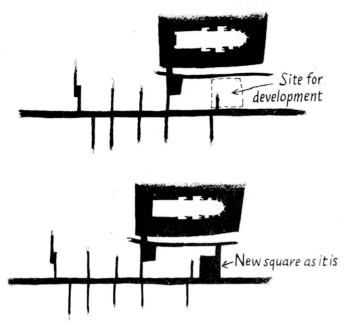

Site for development

New square as it is

New square as it might have been

The arrangement and organisation of spaces over a wide area also affects the appearance of individual buildings. In Canterbury the cathedral, the most important building in the city, is given greater impact and a special relationship to the High Street by the arrangement of space around it. The views out of the High Street are blocked, maintaining the enclosure of the street and almost hiding the cathedral from view, photograph above, so that the cathedral is only seen in full when one has left the High Street, passed through a small square, and penetrated the archway into the cathedral close.

Further up the High Street, photograph left, new development ignores the local disciplines and opens up a bald view to the cathedral, thus removing some of its mystery. The three plans show the original situation, what happened, and what might have happened.

167

The narrow Lanes at Brighton, covering a considerable part of the town centre, contrast with the more formal layout of roads around. New development, plan below, has maintained the tight enclosure of the Lanes and their domestic scale.

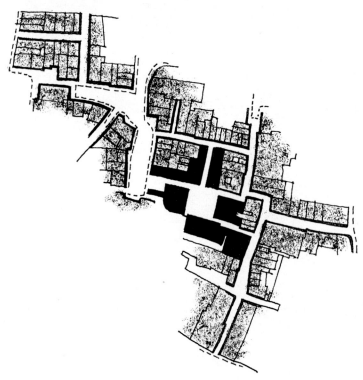

Facing page, top: this is how the village of Thaxted, Essex, has developed up to the present day, with recent development contributing nothing to the old settlement, nor respecting its arrangement of spaces. New housing has created its own spaces—shading diagrams show overall pattern—larger than the more important historic central ones: the buildings turn their backs on and divorce themselves from the existing village. The relationship of town to landscape is also blurred.

Lower drawings: examining the existing townscape, and noting the importance of the central spaces, new development might have retained the original significance. Here is an example of how it might have been. The central spaces remain dominant and new development is subservient to them.

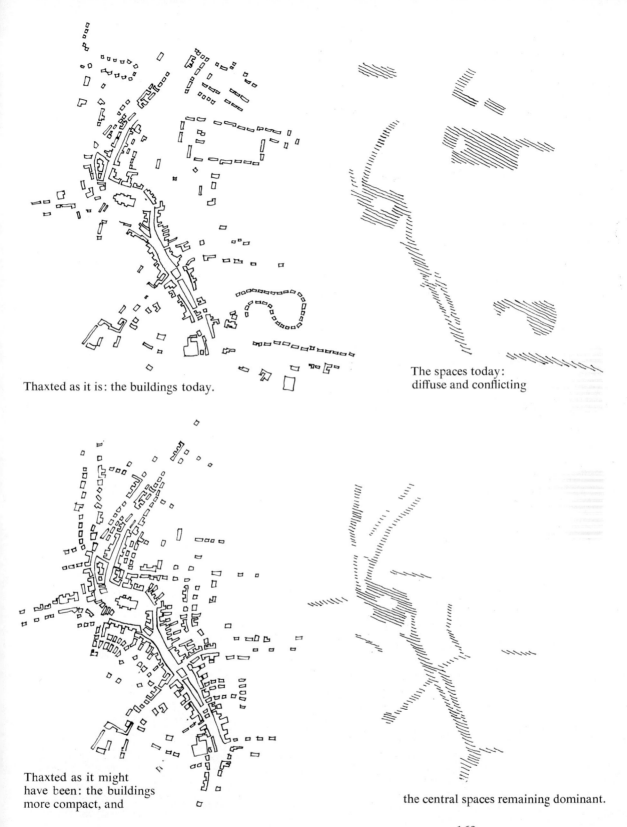

Thaxted as it is: the buildings today.

The spaces today:
diffuse and conflicting

Thaxted as it might
have been: the buildings
more compact, and

the central spaces remaining dominant.

Siting of Multi-storey Car Parks

The siting of large new buildings does not concern only the street in which they are placed. The whole grain of the town is often affected by them. In many cases, the bulk of the buildings, particularly of multi-storey car parks, disrupts the scale and skyline of the surrounding town-scape. In Shrewsbury this car park still seems too massive for the scale of the area despite attempts to break up the bulk of the building.

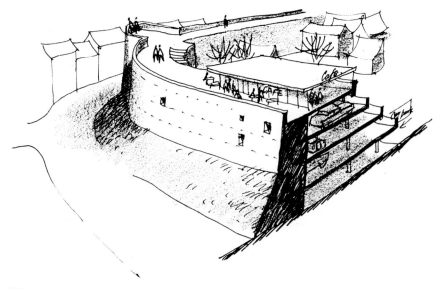

There are many possibilities for inserting multi-storey car parks into a town. Using the natural rise and fall of the land can help to provide unobtrusive sites, for example. The sketch, left, shows one example of how a town wall might be used to aid the assimilation of the structures into a town's fabric.

The massing of most towns and cities builds up to the centre where a town-hall, cathedral or church is usually the dominant feature, left. If the town is to retain its character this build-up of scale to one or two buildings of social significance must be maintained.

Centre drawing: here a large bulky car park builds up the scale in the wrong place, disrupting the grain of the town. It is always more satisfactory to aim for car parks in smaller units, distributed in such a way as to maintain the inherent build up of scale of the town, bottom drawing.

Multi-storey car parks are usually visually more acceptable than open-ground car parks which tear open the fabric of the town. In the sketch, below, a multi-storey car park picks up the scale of the street and maintains the building line. See also drawing at foot of facing page.

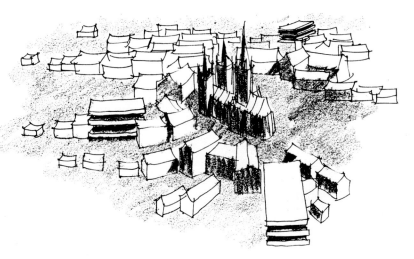

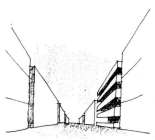

171

Design of Infilling

The effective preservation of one building or group of buildings will not only make demands on the other planning policies but will also affect the renewal and redevelopment of neighbouring sites and the quality of architecture of new buildings. But within his client's brief, the architect has the right to design as he believes appropriate. He usually defends this right vigorously, though on occasion he has been known to sell it.

In historic towns there is a public interest beyond that of client or architectural inventiveness. No developer or architect has the right to destroy the quality of an ancient street or the setting of an historic building. This does not concern only the building next door and the need to design in sympathy with it. The new building must be influenced by the qualities of the whole group of buildings into which it must fit.

The test of what comprises a group will be the degree to which the buildings combine to form a visual whole. It will therefore include all those buildings which are seen together and which interact visually to create a single image or scene. This will obviously include a single row of buildings on one side of the street, and it might also include opposite sides of a street or the sides of a square and, in some cases, be extended to include several streets. In each case the combination of buildings creates an overall visual completeness which acts as a cohesive discipline.

All too many architects neglect this aspect of design. In the first instance therefore this is a matter for education. The architect's training ought to include a course on the design of infilling; few schools of architecture deal with this subject at present. Where clients are concerned, publications by local authorities can be instructive and useful to the architect in persuading his client that he, too, must accept some aesthetic limitations. Some local authorities already issue illustrated pamphlets to guide the design of new development.

The overall architectural character of streets has in nearly every case come about simply because architects and builders in the past have not copied previous styles but built according to the ideas of their own age. Looking at any street in a town which has grown slowly over the centuries, one is immediately impressed by the way in which styles of architecture have changed and developed and materials have been used in different ways. To copy past styles is therefore not the answer.

There will always be a temporary difference between old and new—the effect of age on existing buildings will make the new stand out from the old. Cleaning old buildings and generally avoiding new materials that will not weather, can help. Some modern buildings never age; their materials are

172

hard or glazed and their colours are such that the passing of time has very little effect on them (certainly that is the claim of the manufacturers). Even the most sympathetic new buildings require time and a patina of age to enable them to fit comfortably into old surroundings.

No design policy can of course cope with different architectural appreciation or taste. But in the same way that the architect accepts a brief from his client and is influenced by the existing landscape, so his design must be influenced by the existing neighbouring buildings. He must look for, or be provided with, a visual discipline as part of his brief. It must be a flexible discipline which does not corset the imagination and it must be used and interpreted creatively. It should not set out to influence style and it will generally be used only where a number of existing buildings are to be preserved within a group.

The function of the discipline will vary according to circumstances. In a street with only a few buildings worth preserving and where change is to take place quickly it cannot be applied rigidly. The new buildings which will predominate must create their own group discipline to a large extent.

However pleasingly this building in Maidstone had been designed, its use as a car park on the upper floors probably means it is fundamentally unsuitable for a conservation area. Building use is the first consideration in the design of infilling.

173

As an instrument of elevational control the design discipline will only be of value under certain conditions. The use to which the buildings are put and the pressure for change or expansion of use in a particular area will radically affect the degree to which it can be successful. Clearly the most meticulous check list of neighbouring qualities will be of little use if, for example, a garage must be sited in the middle of a row of residential properties; the garage will never acquire the right domestic qualities. There will be a point at which the check list becomes meaningless, either in relation to the scale of new development and changes of use, or to the speed of change.

The rigid application of building regulations and planning standards will usually act against successful infilling in a group of buildings. Provisions in relation to day-lighting angles, floor heights and window openings, for example, will need to be administered sympathetically, bearing in mind the characteristics of the group of buildings as a whole.

Where there are large numbers of properties under single ownership (usually a good indication of pressure for change), planning applications will be bound to centre on large-scale developments to replace the smaller units. Where these pressures for change cannot be deflected to other sites and the scale of development is clearly too great to create the right setting for the older buildings, the area must be considered comprehensively in three dimensions. The old street concept may need to be given up and the use of a check list of group quality abandoned with it. An entirely new handling of spaces may be required if the few really good old buildings are to remain in a sympathetic setting of suitable scale. Here the local authority may have to co-operate closely with the developers and may itself need to promote development to ensure a suitable assembly of land of the right size and at the right time.

The work that must be done to prepare the group design brief for the practising architect and his client may well be carried out as part of the work of development control. But it must be remembered that it is work that only an architect can do effectively, and there is something to be said for the same person or persons carrying out all stages of visual and historic survey and appraisal to attain the same aesthetic judgement throughout— part of the character of towns comes from this visual completeness.

Development control will be needed whilst wider policies are being worked out. The architect, having identified the buildings that might be preserved at an early stage in the planning process, might draw up a preliminary check list of group qualities to be maintained, which with his continued advice those involved in development control could apply in the interim.

A problem often arises where a County Council is proposing an Urban Structure Map or Local Plan and broad policies for conservation, but the

174

District Council has delegated powers of development control and will in fact implement planning schemes. Whilst the County Council must lay down general design policies the local Council will need strong architectural advice if it is to administer a Conservation Policy. Where the need arises a small team of architects might be set up on a permanent basis, at County Council level, offering specialist conservation advice to District Councils either as a free county service, or for a fee payable to the County Council.

As soon as time permits, the detailed brief or discipline for each group of buildings should be published. If the brief is to be effective as a discipline it must be made known to developers and the general public in advance. Few people will willingly change the basic appearance of a design after it has been conceived.

Any such brief must therefore be publicised as far in advance of receiving planning applications as possible. It might best be set out in pamphlet form or alternatively be available in the District or Borough Council's offices. The use of the code will of course be most necessary in Conservation Areas, but other areas could be considered as well.

Often the decision to preserve a building will have been coloured by the feeling that a new building could not replace qualities in themselves quite indifferent; sometimes simply age itself. Considerations of use and viability apart, it may be felt that a building of no great architectural quality is so important to a group of buildings that preservation is imperative. It will be noticed that some buildings in the Ministry of Housing and Local Government's lists of historic buildings have been given a grading that reflects their group value, a grading higher than they would normally warrant on architectural merit. This implies that a new building would adversely affect the appearance of the group of buildings as a whole, and therefore consideration should be given to the preservation of the building for its group value. But to preserve such a building can be a strong condemnation of the sensitivity of the architect and his ability to design in sympathy with surrounding buildings. Listing these buildings also tends to devalue the existing buildings of real quality.

By the use of the design discipline for infilling, and by paying close attention to the qualities of surrounding buildings, better and more sensitive design can be achieved for new buildings. This will reduce the need for preserving buildings of relatively low quality. It should, however, be remembered that most towns do not illustrate one specific period of time. Their value as old towns is that they show history as a continuous process with different periods and styles of architecture slowly building up to create the powerful sense of historic growth which so many of our towns have today. New buildings also have a part to play in this story.

The Ministry of Housing lists of buildings of architectural and historic

175

importance or interest—which are constantly being revised—seldom cover effectively the last hundred or hundred and fifty years. The local planning authority, which can draw up its own lists, should consider which additional buildings are worthy of preservation in the light of the need to maintain the sense of historic change up to the present day. This further consideration might result in a wider Conservation Policy with less opportunity for the construction of new buildings. It may also mean that most of the buildings on the Ministry's supplementary lists need preserving with as much care as those on the statutory lists.

One of the most difficult tasks in a conservation area is to design new buildings which fit in with the existing groups of buildings.

How do we identify a group of buildings where new development should be influenced by the appearance of the whole? Such a group may be identified by its overall historic associations or by a local style of building. Most often it will be marked simply by the cohesive appearance of all the buildings when seen together. There will usually be a considerable number of listed buildings which must be preserved, and the setting of which ought to be sympathetically maintained. On these two pages are three examples of groups of buildings where new development ought to be required to maintain the visual cohesion of the group as a whole; many of the individual buildings would be preserved. Facing page: South Street, Durham; above, Fishpool Street, St. Albans; below: Allergate, Durham. Clearly, each group has a visual continuity but there is also a continuity of use and scale and type of activity which must be maintained in infilling.

The group to be considered may consist of one side of a street—particularly if it is seen on a curve, top drawing. Often, the group will involve both sides of a street, centre drawing, or perhaps three or more sides, bottom drawing; always all the buildings seen together in a single view.

The qualities that make a group of buildings, that give it visual cohesion, are as many and as various as the groups that exist. No two groups of building look alike.

The group above, Barn Hill in Stamford, is given its overall quality by the mixture and irregularity of individual buildings, and this is the most common type to be found in our towns. There are, however, two other groups that also need to be considered:

the terrace or architectural entity; and the group with units which are individual but are built in the same style or the same period. We first examine these three different types of group and the approach we must adopt towards them, and then study the various qualities which together create their character. These qualities can be set down in a simple check list which can be used in the design discipline.

179

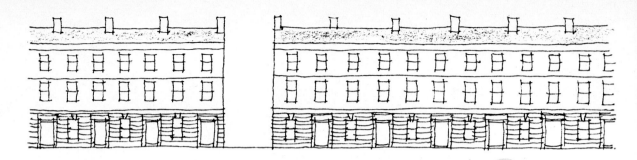

The Terrace

Where a group of buildings has been designed as an architectural entity, above, there is little choice but to rebuild any single unit of that design to match exactly the existing façade—to reinstate the same proportion of window to wall, the same height, the same materials and detailing. Here the check list of architectural quality works as a strict discipline upon the architect. The solution will generally be to rebuild a facsimile, like the restoration at Bath, left.

Part of this main shopping street in Torquay is composed of a long terrace of properties, designed on a curve as a single architectural entity. Rebuilding of a single unit here, for example, might well repeat the same architectural design.

Exceptions to the Rule

There are always exceptions to such rigid controls over elevational design. Where a new terrace must face an old terrace across a square, the new building —still maintaining the right sense of formal enclosure—might be quite different architecturally. In Newcastle, below left, a library neatly abuts a long terrace of 19th century houses—both good buildings of their own time, but sitting happily together. Notice the effective transition between old and new: a simple brick structure mediates between brick terrace and steel and glass.

In Dorset Square, London, below right, a glass-walled office block joins a distinguished 18th century terrace. By expressing the staircases on the façade, and recessing them into the main wall surface, the new is kept just separate from the old.

Similar Period—Individual Buildings

Infilling in groups like the one shown above, requires the greatest care of all in design and detailing. Each existing building in the group will have been designed individually, yet to a standard book of rules. Such groups, usually of the 18th century, became virtually one of the earliest types of system building in this country. The same details were repeated in almost every town but were of course executed by different craftsmen, resulting in a high degree of individual interpretation within the limits of the system. In most cases, new buildings will need to adopt at least the same formality of style, and in many instances a similar proportion of window to wall. Eaves height may vary slightly and in some cases materials also. In St. Martin's, Stamford, below, a group of buildings, each constructed separately but in the same period and style, forms a strong visual group.

183

East Castle Street, Bridgenorth.

In Ludlow, an unspectacular answer to the problem, quietly filling in a gap in a group of Georgian houses; perhaps the small windows could have been taller and narrower.

The General Dental Council's buildings in Wimpole Street, London, above, is a modern reinterpretation of 18th century architecture; on the upper floors almost a copy of a past elevational style, but still recognisable as a modern building.

Left: an attempt at infilling in St. Martin's, Stamford. The right proportion of window to wall, but the building really needed a pitched roof.

Mixed Group of Different Periods

An example, above, of the mixture of different types of buildings which have grown up over the centuries and which combine to create an interesting, varied and yet somehow integrated street scene. There is a mixture of materials, window size, height and width of buildings.

186

A group of shops in York, above, and another in Salisbury, facing page, both illustrate well the mixture of architectural period and styles that is so common in many of our towns. There are, however, two factors from which their visual quality has arisen. Firstly, the use of buildings has in the past often varied within a single street, resulting in a variety of designs. Secondly, the buildings have taken on local qualities in design and detailing and have often been altered by successive generations. Left: infilling in a mixed group in Petersfield. Notice how the top floor of the building has been divided into a number of large dormers, to break up the outline and maintain the variety.

In some streets, the greater the diversity of uses, within a broadly compatible range, that can be retained the livelier the street architecture will be. Some towns will have quite distinct areas associated with particular uses. Here are some examples of buildings which bring variety to the streets in which they are placed. Left: the Old Market Hall, Scarborough; below: the Gas Works, Dolgellau; facing page: change of scale and function in Victoria Street, London.

188

From here to p. 213 the qualities that bring continuity to a group of buildings are illustrated under several headings.

1. Building Line

The plan shape or building line is the basis of the continuity of a group of buildings. The line of façades along a street or around a space will condition the way the individual buildings are seen and the relationship between one building and the next.

In Shrewsbury, above, the changing building line creates some points of interest on both sides of the street. The sketch shows how this interest would be lost if two properties were redeveloped without any reference to quality of the building line. Not only would the group be less interesting, but the street as a whole would be opened up, losing its sense of enclosure.

Also in Shrewsbury, in Swan Hill, above, the slight variation in building line affords a fuller view of some individual buildings and thus creates an interesting street scene. Other buildings are hidden from view until one has moved along the street. The sketch shows a way in which pavements can be kept to a consistent width, while retaining the building line.

In some cases a firm uniform building line can determine the character of a street. In Birmingham, left, New Street has a truly city atmosphere due to the height of the buildings and the straight, formal building line.

191

2. Building Height and Skyline

One of the most difficult visual characteristics to maintain in a group of buildings is height and skyline. Most of our older shopping streets were constructed to three or four storeys with pitched roofs and chimneys to break up the skyline. New shops do not require much space above first floor level and certainly do not often need chimneys or gables.

The High Street at Guildford, left, would suffer disastrously from a lowering of the building height, as shown in the drawing below.

A street with interesting rooflines in Scarborough, in which an imaginary new large scale development, drawing below left, flattens out the broken skyline despite a desperate attempt to decorate it. Additional and varied uses above first floor level, right hand drawing, might provide a more sculptural building.

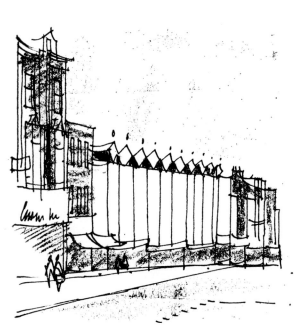

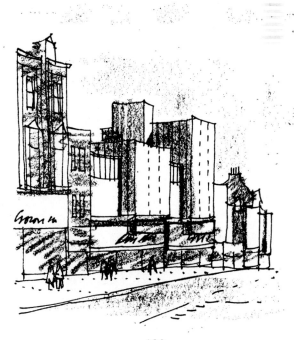

This new building in Horsham required extra space on upper floors, which were set back from the street façade in order to reduce the apparent height of the building.

In Birmingham, a new building was set back on a low podium from the building line, destroying the continuity of the group.

In Tonbridge the first floor of a shop is set back, breaking up the continuity of skyline.

In Sloane Street, London, large box-like balconies give added interest to the skyline of this block of flats. Notice how the bay windows break up the length of the façade.

In Horsham, two clearly separate buildings line up at parapet level, producing a dull skyline and increasing the apparent length of the building. The street is largely made up of small properties.

A shop in Marlborough, below left, picks up the local tradition of gables. (The building on its right has now been demolished.) Reusing local forms and traditions in this way is often a useful means of maintaining the continuity of the street elevation. Care should be taken to ensure that such features are not mere elevational tricks but are integral parts of the building's conception and construction.

The broken eaves line of this building in Skipton, left, breaks up an otherwise hard silhouette.
A more positive skyline and less of a gimmick than the raised windows in Skipton, buildings in Cirencester, below, break up the eaves line more functionally to produce a more domestic scale.

3. Width of Unit

In thriving shopping streets, large building units and windows are a feature of modern retail practice; where once all the shops were narrow, new ones have appeared which take three or four times the width of the old. By breaking up the façades into bays and attempting to model the wall surface with a vertical emphasis, the new can be blended more successfully with the old—providing the bays reflect the internal arrangement and function of rooms.

The small section of Lewes High Street has quite wide units, some of which are not yet converted into shops.

Pressures for redevelopment might well produce the kind of shop shown in the sketch: long and hard-edged, destroying the domestic scale of the street.

An excellent example of infilling in a group of houses in Cheyne Walk, London, above. It repeats the same size of building unit and the same domestic scale by breaking the façade with balcony recesses. Left: Culpeper Court, Walnut Tree Walk, Lambeth, a good example of new development adjoining an existing terrace, maintaining the form and continuity of the group. In this case there is a horizontal emphasis to be maintained.

A design for infilling in Chester. Notice how the upper storeys are split into vertical bays to reduce the apparent size of the building. Incidentally, the continuance of the 'Rows' perpetuates an historic tradition.

New buildings in the village of Bletchingley, Surrey, are broken up into smaller units to reduce the apparent size of the development.

The horizontal emphasis on the façade of this building in Devizes is far too strong for the street. A stronger expression of the party wall, carrying it up to the skyline, would have broken up the width of the unit.

4. Quality of Detailing and Materials

The prevalence of a traditional local building material can give a strong sense of unity to a town. Buildings well constructed in the local vernacular should be strong candidates for preservation. Similarly, it is often possible to maintain the same materials in new buildings, where the tradition can be reinterpreted to modern structural requirements. Above left: flints and brick in Brighton. Above right: Stone in Haworth. Below left: tile hanging in Tenterden, Kent. Below right: timber cladding, tile and brick in Tenterden.

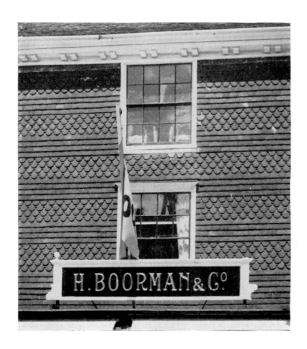

Care should be taken to see not only that traditional materials are used, but that they are used in the right way. In a stone district, for example, where stone has in the past been used structurally, new buildings would be better constructed in some other material of similar colour or texture, than with the stone used as a thin veneer over a brick or concrete block structure. Despite the use of expensive stone for the walls of this bungalow it still looks out of place in a Cotswold village where simplicity is the order of the day. The tiled roof and weatherboarding do not fit in with the stone walls. The stone coursing is also too formal.

The quality and character of detailing can often be more important to the group than the material used. This terrace in Lewes has a unity of appearance which is due almost entirely to the quality of its detailing: the same shallow perforation of the wall by windows throughout, the brick structure clearly and simply stated and the strong vertical emphasis—all these characteristics draw it together as a single unit. Notice how the eaves-line rises slightly for each building.
A new building with a different type of structure and materials could disrupt the continuity of the group. Dropping the eaves-line also destroys the rhythm of the buildings.

In Reading a new building stands out from its neighbours because the detailing is timid and flat. A building with plenty of modelling on the façade, whether in brick, stone or concrete, would have been better in the context of the original Victorian group (the group has now been almost entirely redeveloped).

Alongside St. Katharine's Dock, London, a concrete building captures the spirit of the surrounding brick warehouses by creating an impression of solidity and thickness.

These flats are seen from St. James's Place, above, and Green Park, below. From St. James's Place the building is scaled down in apparent width and in detailing: it suits the small scale of the street. The marble, bronze and glass fit well with the stuccoed terraces because they have been used at the right domestic scale and therefore have the same visual impact as the surrounding buildings.

From Green Park the scale of the building increases with that of its neighbours, and it asserts itself as a single unit, just like the others in the group.

Above left: stone used effectively in Oxford. Another building in Oxford, above right, which picks up the same quality of detailing as the rest of the group.

Sometimes a contrast in quality of detailing can be effective. A good example of infilling in Pride Hill,

Shrewsbury, below. While the general scale of the street is maintained, the new building contrasts in quality of detailing with the buildings on either side. The architect has observed the existing qualities and introduced a more rugged modelling similar to that of the buildings further up the street.

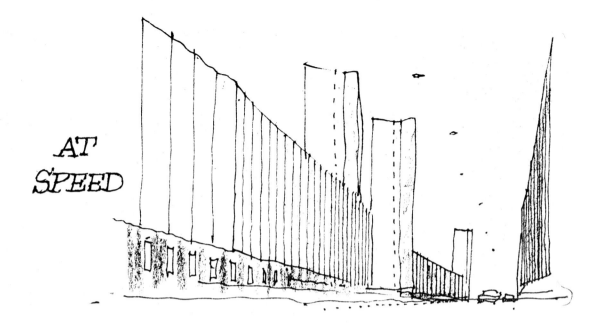

AT
SPEED

The faster the speed of movement of the viewer, the more important the massing of buildings becomes and the less the need for details to look at, above. Where there is a slow speed of movement, in a pedestrian area for example, detailing needs to be more intricate, providing more visual interest, below

WALKING

207

Here are two different places: the seaside at Brighton and the riverside of the Thames in London, which, because of their functions and the different traditions of design approach, each take on an individual design discipline. In one place the discipline is light and fanciful, in the other hard and strong. These basic qualities ought to affect the design of buildings in the areas.

The materials of the façades of buildings are not of course the only surfaces which need attention. The repaving of streets and squares should either continue the local tradition or, depending on the mood of the place, create positive new qualities of texture. In many old towns different textures were used to indicate the situation of different activities and a study of the use of paving can produce a discipline for modern development in the area.

Existing paving that is worth retaining, Lymington, Hampshire, top. New paving in a simple design at Stevenage, centre, and more decorative treatment at Dorking, bottom.

5. Proportion of Window to Wall

Most existing groups of buildings seem to have a continuous and regular proportion of window to wall throughout. New methods of trading demand larger window sizes and these need careful handling if the continuity of the group is not to be destroyed.

A new shop in Shrewsbury, left, with a fragment of the old building embedded in its façade, floats uncomfortably on plate glass.

A new shop in Chichester, Sussex, below, still has large windows but manages to support the weight above adequately.

In York, a neat conversion,
lower picture, that retains the
supporting columns for the
upper storey yet provides greatly
improved window display.

An uncomfortably large ground floor opening in a group of buildings in a Cotswold village, Charlbury.
In Chessel's Court, Canongate, Edinburgh, below left, and in Cumbernauld, below right, new buildings maintain the same proportion of window to wall as their neighbours. . .

. . . which is more than can be said for this shop at Bridgnorth, left. Effective infilling in Winchester, below, with the right proportion of window to wall on the first floor.

In many cases new buildings will be so large that their size alone will make them incompatible with the existing street scene. New development in Shrewsbury, above, is quite out of scale with the existing façades.

In Grimsby, below, a new large building disrupts the scale and creates no sense of space or enclosure in the street.

Sometimes the larger units can be inserted at the rear of the existing street. Their scale can provide occasional exciting contrasts when glimpsed down alleyways or passages.

In Guildford a large multi-storey car park makes an impact by its contrast of scale to the High Street. This view down a narrow alleyway by the church is admittedly flattering to a building which is in many other respects disastrous to the townscape.

Large scale development at the rear.

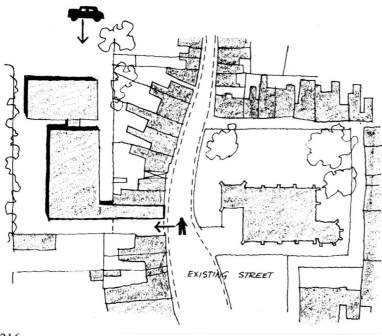

EXISTING STREET

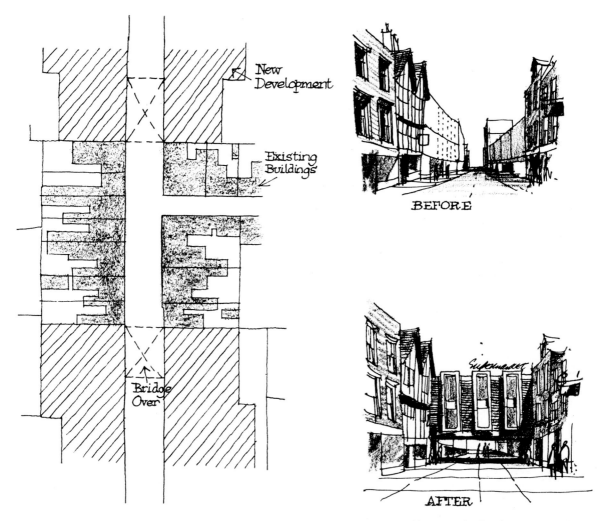

New Development

Existing Buildings

BEFORE

Bridge Over

AFTER

Large scale development shielded.

Facing page: one way of masking the effects of new large scale development in a small town is to retain some of the small buildings as a visual buffer between old and new. Vehicular access to new development should not be opened up from the old part of the town, but should be away from the historic area, perhaps also with a pedestrian access-way through from the original street.

This page: where pressure for change is very great and new buildings would inevitably be bulky, an entirely new setting might be created for the smaller scale historic buildings. The new buildings might span the existing street, creating new small scale spaces, shielding the new buildings from the old and creating a new setting for them.

217

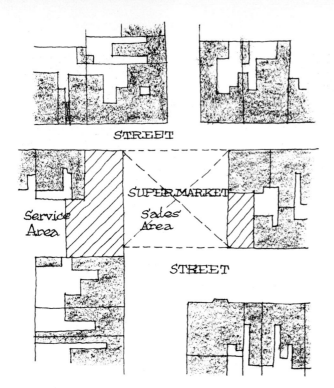

STREET

SUPERMARKET
Sales
Area

Service
Area

STREET

One way of incorporating large-scale developments into Conservation Areas is to use their interiors as part of the overall arrangement of spaces in the town centre. Here the sales space of a supermarket takes on the quality of a covered market square, the pedestrian seeing right through the building into the street beyond.

Large scale development expressed.

Where there is a gap in a formal
terrace a new building, quite
different in architectural form
and scale, can provide a focal
point which complements the
existing layout.

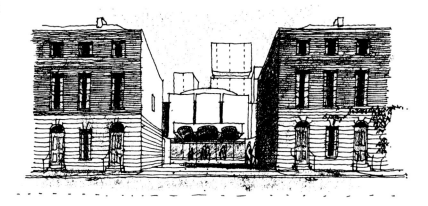

Tidying up

The difference
between old and new
can be sometimes
overcome by washing
the old buildings.
Much can also be
achieved by schemes
to remove clutter,
and tidy up street
furniture. For
example, this street
in Glasgow could
obviously benefit
from a
rationalisation of
street furniture.

219

Face-lift schemes can play an important part in improving the quality of the street. One of the problems connected with these schemes is that it is very easy to lose individuality and local traditions of advertising and colour. Face-lifts can too often result in the removal of old styles of lettering and their replacement by inferior plastic cut-outs. Examples like these two might be well worth retaining where such a scheme is envisaged

Finally, if there are going to be schemes to brighten things up, don't go mad.

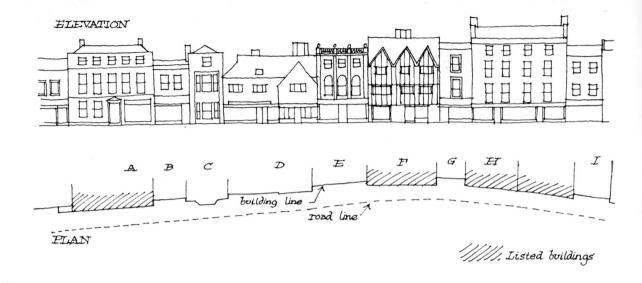

ELEVATION

A   B   C   D   E   F   G H   I

building line

road line

PLAN

///// Listed buildings

Application of the Design Discipline for Infilling

The sketches on these two pages and page 224 illustrate the results of the application of design discipline. No allowance is made here for the timing of development which might take place over several years. In studying the examples it will be appreciated that control of building use is an essential and complementary part of the discipline.

The drawing above shows the street elevation as it might be surveyed. The group to be considered is one side of a street and is a mixture of individual buildings of different sizes and of different periods. The main quality is variety. The predominant use is shopping with building 'A' used for office accommodation. Upper floors are also generally used for offices with occasional flats. There are several buildings worthy of preservation.

Top of facing page: the street in perspective as it is today. The group qualities, which would normally be described in more detail, are as follows:
Building Line is broken. Individual buildings step back from the general building line, which follows the curve of the road. A number of flank walls break up the street elevation and the curve tends to foreshorten the elevations from various viewpoints. Building 'E' almost disappears from view in perspective.
Building Height is varied, the maximum difference between buildings being about 12′ 0″. No two buildings adjoining have the same eaves height. There is more variation in the heights of buildings between 'A' and 'F' than there is in the rest of the group.
Skyline is broken but there is little detail against the sky.

Quality of Detailing and Materials. There is a mixture of various materials with a tendency to more intricate detailing around buildings 'E' and 'F'.
Size of Unit varies and, with the exception of building 'D', there is a strong vertical emphasis in the elevations, even more pronounced in perspective. This verticality is less apparent at the ends of the group due to the curve of the street.
Proportion of Window to Wall varies but buildings 'A', 'B', 'G', 'H', and 'I' all have a similar proportion.

Centre of facing page illustrates the effect of development which ignores the variety of the existing group quality and has been carried out without the use of a design discipline. Buildings 'A', 'F' and 'I' are retained.

The development generally flattens the building height at too low a level, leaving the older buildings standing above the new eaves height. The eaves-lines create a monotonous skyline. On the other hand, the nearest building is too high and almost lines up with building 'A'. The proportion of window to wall in the new buildings is not satisfactory; the windows are too large. The building line is flattened out and the flank walls of individual buildings have been lost, removing much of the street's modelling and visual interest.

Bottom of facing page: new development influenced by the design discipline, creating a similar visual quality to that of the existing street and a more suitable setting for the older buildings. Whilst the architectural style of individual buildings may not win prizes, the important thing is that the street retains a visual continuity.

Here is shown the effect of large-scale development which overpowers the older buildings. This might well be a case where, if the pressure for change cannot be diverted elsewhere, the street concept itself might be changed (as suggested on page 217).

This drawing illustrates the masking of new, large scale development from old by changing the concept of the street into a series of traffic-free squares.

V. SURVEY AND APPRAISAL

The Approach

This chapter outlines a check list for a survey method and techniques of appraisal. The survey is the first stage of the planning process for both preservation and change. However, before deciding upon the contents of a visual and historic survey we must determine the objectives of the survey and the way it will be used in relation to the preparation of a Conservation Policy. There is no point in gathering unnecessary quantities of information. As the pressures for change and the characters of towns differ, any outline of survey, such as is given here, can only be a general guide. A large town may be tackled as a number of areas, perhaps according to the age of buildings or the visual completeness of certain parts or areas of specific activity. A small town or village will be considered as a whole.

Generally the smaller the area the more detailed the approach must be and the more the design and siting of individual buildings will matter. The kind of survey that would be needed in a town like Buxton or Leamington, where there is a strong architectural unity, will have a different emphasis from that in an ordinary market town with fewer listed buildings.

A visual survey in an industrial town of no real architectural quality, might be based more on social organisation; it might attempt to discover the way in which social focal points—schools, shops and pubs for example—are expressed visually, so that redevelopment maintains the same community bonds. The character of the town will therefore broadly determine the type of survey and its contents. There are two basic methods of approach to survey. The first may be called the personal or subjective approach; the second the democratic or objective approach. Neither, by itself, is perfect.

The subjective approach is the result of one person (usually the architect) looking at a town and assessing in an intuitive way, the visual and historic qualities that make up the town's identity. This assessment will, of course, be backed by archaeological evidence and by such historical documents and lists of buildings of architectural and historic interest as are available.

The objective approach attempts to identify visual qualities by testing public reaction to the environment, conducting a kind of opinion poll to find out what people notice most about their town, what they like and dislike.

The subjective approach is open to abuse because the taste of one person is often too obscure or biased to be a guide to useful visual standards. The objective approach has the obvious flaw that people are conditioned to accepting their environment, whatever its quality, because they have got used to it. It is perhaps also true that most of our efforts to conserve the fabric of our towns would be unnecessary if more people valued and fully understood the quality of their towns. Whatever the approach, the burden of establishing a town's visual and historic qualities will, however, rest finally with the architect on the planning team.

Kevin Lynch, in his book *The Image of the City*,* considers " . . . the visual quality of the American city by studying the mental image of that city which is held by its citizens". The book concentrates "especially on one particular visual quality: the apparent clarity or legibility of the cityscape". Although the results of surveys described in the book are not concerned with any precise definition of architectural quality or value, they illustrate considerable similarities between verbal interviews to ascertain city image, and field studies carried out by trained observers which attempt to predict the results of such verbal interviews. The objective approach can therefore help to confirm a broad subjective survey or it may be used in the beginning to establish the framework for detailed study. A local civic society may be able to help in conducting verbal interviews.

It is useful to carry out a simple reconnaissance to establish the main visual and historic features of a town. A full and detailed survey would then follow giving priority to particular parts or aspects of the town which were under immediate pressure and for which planning schemes were urgently required. A reconnaissance in most smaller towns will however reveal that the pressures are widespread and the character of the town comes from a variety of sources. A complete survey covering the whole town might well be indispensable. This chapter sets out to describe such a survey and to place it in the context of a normal planning appraisal.

It should be made quite clear that this will not mean embarking on a programme of several years' work. A trained eye, spending quite a short time in the field, will pick out the majority of qualities which are important. It needs to be emphasised that a visual survey of a town must be based on field studies, not carried out from an office, but time spent later in carefully noting down and describing the qualities found, will be invaluable.

Aerial photographs can help to clarify first impressions and give an appreciation of the form of the town. Rough diagrammatic models, illustrating local topography and the massing of development, may also assist in the visual survey. But it must be remembered that people never experience towns from the air, only by being in the streets, and there are consequently fascinations and dangers in using these aids.

The chart, (No. 1, on page 227) lists the various items of survey that might be covered and the policy aims which stem from particular aspects of survey. The order of survey, as shown on this chart, is chosen to

---

* See Bibliography.

226

Chart 1.

Main Survey Items

- Views from outside. Urban boundaries
- Views out to countryside
- Views across the town
- Focal points
- Listed buildings. Permanent buildings
- Groups of buildings
- Areas of predominantly greater scale
- Local identity areas
- Major identity areas
- Archaeological features
- Road layout
- Space and enclosure
- Areas of opportunity

Design Disciplines / Allied Surveys

TOWN/LANDSCAPE RELATIONSHIP

- Quality of landscape and types (woodland, heath, etc.)
- Agricultural value of land
- Flood plains
- Land capable of drainage
- Footpaths and public open spaces
- Current planning proposals and applications

HIGH BUILDINGS POLICY

- Load-bearing capacity of ground
- Effect of concentration of uses on traffic generation
- Current planning proposals and applications

THE DESIGN OF INFILLING

- Condition of buildings
- Building and site values
- Ownership and demand for use
- Current planning proposals and applications

CONSERVATION AREAS

- Historical and archaeological background
- Condition of buildings
- Grants already given
- Ownership and demand for use
- Building and site value
- Environmental improvements required; resiting of unsuitable uses
- Current planning proposals and applications

TOWNSCAPE DISCIPLINE

- Historical and archaeological background
- Major needs for change; roads, car parks, etc.
- Current planning proposals and applications

facilitate the grouping of the survey items into different sections of policy. It does not follow that the surveys would be carried out in that order, nor does it follow that any one item of survey is necessarily more important than another. The importance of individual items of survey will be governed by the qualities of the town under consideration.

A number of other closely allied surveys might need to be carried out in association with the visual survey and the various policy aims. These will provide information not necessarily required in the normal course of other planning work. Some of these are suggested on Chart 2. The surveys and policy aims must now be seen in the framework of the planning process.

Chart No. 2 sets out a method of work in five stages illustrating the testing of conservation and its interaction with other planning aims:

Stage 1. The *visual and historic survey* (the contents as outlined on Chart 1) is shown as a parallel survey to other planning surveys (e.g. traffic and land-use surveys).

Stage 2. The *first appraisal* of policy aims is drawn up, conservation aims running parallel with other local planning and regional aims.

Stage 3. The policy aims for conservation are *tested* for feasibility (associated surveys for each policy aim were outlined on Chart 1) and for compatibility with other planning aims.

Stage 4. The whole range of policy aims are *adjusted* and if necessary alternative aims are examined.

Stage 5. The Conservation Policies can now be confirmed as realistic. Where necessary they are incorporated in the urban structure map or the district or local plans. *Public statements* are made defining the High Buildings Policy and the Design Discipline for Infilling. Conservation Areas may have been designated at an earlier stage, as a temporary measure to safeguard the historic areas. *Action Areas* are identified as part of the overall programme of development for the town and any holding action that is required to safeguard aspects of conservation is carried out.

After testing conservation aims for feasibility or against other planning aims, it may well prove necessary to adjust the various aims, keeping some rather than others. It might be necessary, for example, to abandon a small Conservation Area that it had been hoped to establish, in order to get a stronger Conservation Policy in another area. Similarly, development may be allowed to extend over one part of the countryside which would otherwise have been left open, in order to preserve another of greater visual importance.

It is at this stage that some form of visual or aesthetic grading must take place. This was described in Chapter 2 page 42, under the heading of Selection.

Chart 2. Method of work in drawing up a conservation policy

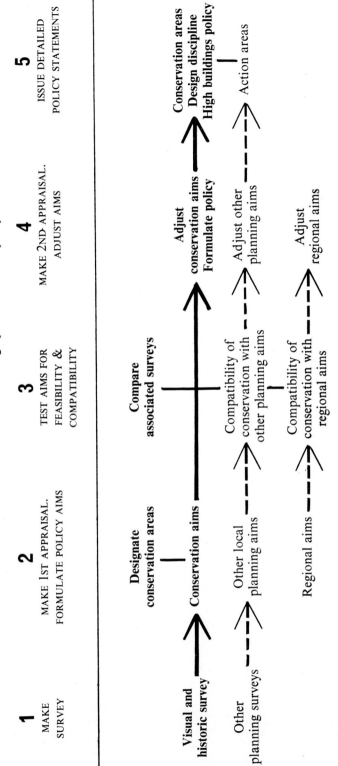

1	**2**	**3**	**4**	**5**
MAKE SURVEY	MAKE 1ST APPRAISAL. FORMULATE POLICY AIMS	TEST AIMS FOR FEASIBILITY & COMPATIBILITY	MAKE 2ND APPRAISAL. ADJUST AIMS	ISSUE DETAILED POLICY STATEMENTS

229

Time taken to carry out this whole process will vary from town to town, according to its size and its existing quality and the local pressures for change. The time taken will also depend upon the speed with which other survey material (traffic and shopping surveys for example) is collected and analysed and the degree to which regional testing is possible. In most planning activity it is now realised that the definitive plan, which closely regulated such things as land-use patterns for periods up to twenty years, is not a realistic way to order the growth and development of a town.

The trend is rather towards statements of policy which can be amended as time passes and conditions change. Conservation is, perhaps, an exception to this trend because it is concerned, in a broad sense, with maintaining the *status quo*. The passing of time and the creation of new pressures for change will not necessarily alter the desirability for conservation, although the problems of achieving it will change if and when the pressures change. Public statements on aspects of Conservation Policy unlike other planning aims, may well hold good for many years; written material, maps and illustrations will therefore cover considerable detail.

The Survey in Detail

The following section outlines the principles of survey and suggests methods of notation for the survey's findings. The studies illustrated here are based on a hypothetical town of approximately 20,000 population. A much larger town might adopt a similar technique but would not necessarily cover the whole town in one exercise. Items of survey are divided into three broad headings: Town/Landscape Relationship (including High Buildings) i.e. the relationship of the town to the countryside; the Townscape; and the Individual Buildings. This divides the survey into three working units, avoiding constant travel between various parts of the town and covering the survey material required for several policy aims in one visit. For example, views from the outside of the town will be required for both Town/Landscape Policy and aspects of High Buildings Policy. Mapped surveys will normally be accompanied by photographs and a written description.

Survey of Town/Landscape Relationship, and High Buildings

OBJECTIVES: To identify the most important features of the existing visual relationship between the town and the landscape.

To identify opportunities for new development which will not detract from the existing relationship or those that may create a completely new image which will enhance the existing relationship.

To identify the existing tall buildings over the town as a whole and the appearance and massing of the built-up areas as a whole.

To suggest areas where new high buildings will not detract from the existing town skylines, or where a positive new skyline might be created.

METHOD: Establish the important viewpoints from which the relationship of town to landscape can be seen and/or which give the most valuable views of the massing and skyline of the town. Views may be taken from country walks or from open spaces, neighbouring towns or villages, from a by-pass or railway line, anywhere in fact where there is an important view to be obtained.

Establish where views are dependent on the movement of the viewer, i.e. where the combination of a number of view-points together make up a significant visual effect.

Mark up on a base map the fields of vision showing the town as a whole, (6 in. or $2\frac{1}{2}$ in. to the mile ordnance survey map will usually be the most convenient scale for towns over 10,000 population).

231

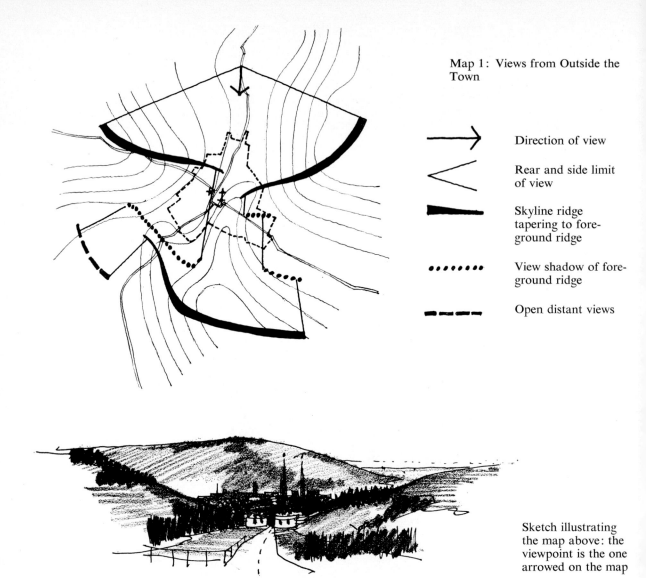

Map 1: Views from Outside the Town

→ Direction of view

〈 Rear and side limit of view

▬ Skyline ridge tapering to foreground ridge

•••••••• View shadow of foreground ridge

▬ ▬ ▬ Open distant views

Sketch illustrating the map above: the viewpoint is the one arrowed on the map

FEATURES TO BE NOTED ON MAP

Views from Outside the Town. Map 1 plots the view from a single viewpoint outside the town. The boundaries of the field of vision are drawn to include the areas of land of which the viewer would normally be conscious, assuming that he would be able to see ahead and from side to side. The sketch illustrates the features of the map and explains the implications of the annotation. (A useful aid to establishing viewpoints and view shadows is a relief model of the local topography with a manœuvrable point source of light. By placing the light source on the viewpoints, the area that is visible will be the same as the area illuminated, but will not, of course, take account of interruptions by buildings or trees).

232

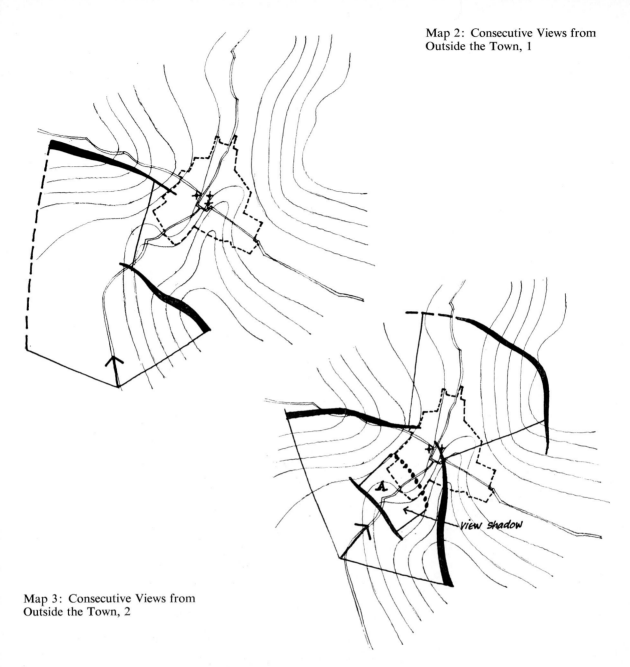

Map 2: Consecutive Views from Outside the Town, 1

Map 3: Consecutive Views from Outside the Town, 2

Consecutive Views from Outside the Town. In this case, the view from outside is important as a combination of consecutive views, and although shown here for clarity on two maps (2 and 3) it might well be completed on a single map. There will usually be more than just two viewpoints to be considered (the visual effect of moving in towards a town was illustrated on page 80). Note the isolated shadow, A, on Map 3. Many areas like this will be found in towns, where small areas are hidden from view by a slight rise in the land form and a consequent foreground ridge.

233

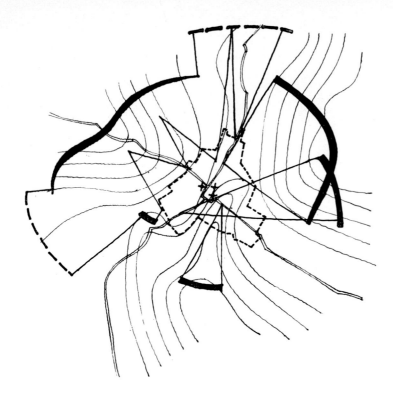

Map 4: Views Out to the
Countryside

Views Out to the Countryside. Here the objectives and method are the
same as those for views from the outside, with the exception that they will
not normally concern the siting of high buildings. There will usually be a
mixture of broad panoramic views (a wide field of vision) and narrow slot
views between buildings (narrow field of vision). See illustrations on pages
78, 91-5.

Map 4 illustrates the variety of views from the main vantage points
within the town looking out towards the countryside. While these main
viewpoints probably give as much detail as is required at this scale, there
will also be individual views from less important places and from private
gardens or upper windows of houses or public buildings (see Map 10 "Views
to Countryside"). These views may need to be protected and they will
normally be considered in the detailed survey of particular areas. However
they may well be important to the Town/Landscape Relationship and
should therefore be considered part of essential survey material in drawing
up policy aims.

234

Map 5: Aims for Town/Landscape Policy and High Buildings Policy

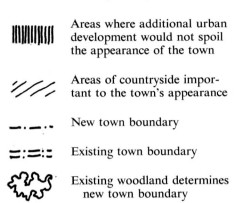

|||||||||| Areas where additional urban development would not spoil the appearance of the town

///// Areas of countryside important to the town's appearance

–·–·· New town boundary

=:=:: Existing town boundary

Existing woodland determines new town boundary

▭ Urban areas where new high buildings should be excluded

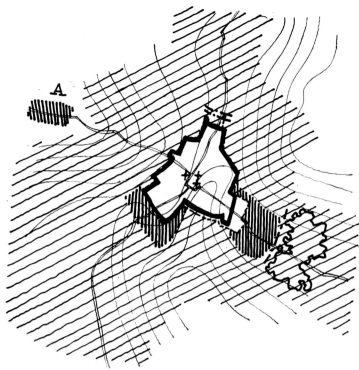

FIRST APPRAISAL OF THE TOWN/LANDSCAPE RELATIONSHIP AND HIGH BUILDINGS

Aims for Town/Landscape Relationship Policy. Map 5 illustrates the first appraisal of town/landscape relationship aims. By a technique of overlays or sieve maps made up of the surveys previously described, areas are shown where development could take place and would remain unseen, or would not spoil views from the principal vantage points. These aims are complemented by areas of countryside which should remain open because they are important to the total image of the town.

In stating these aims it should be remembered that where a town is expanding, new development can create positive new features that could strengthen the visual image of the town. In the appraisal, a new urban fence or town boundary is established in the valley to the east. Similarly, a new satellite village is suggested on the hill to the west at (A). This would remain unseen from most vantage points but might be used as a focal point for the road approaching from the south.

Aims for High Buildings Policy. Also on Map 5 is shown an area from which high buildings ought to be excluded, because the existing skyline is worthy of preservation. Areas not falling within that boundary could be considered for high building development, should there be such a demand. There might well be the opportunity for high, residential buildings in the suggested village settlement to emphasise its role as a focal point.

Had the existing skyline in the town proved to be weak, the appraisal might have reversed the areas defined. The central area would have been

235

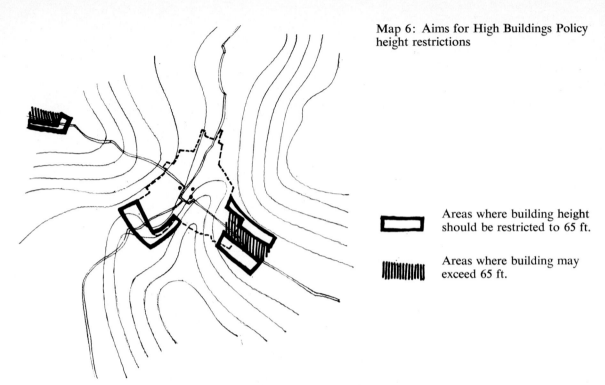

Map 6: Aims for High Buildings Policy
height restrictions

☐ Areas where building height
should be restricted to 65 ft.

|||||||||||| Areas where building may
exceed 65 ft.

the area where new high buildings would be encouraged, and the outer areas would have been those from which high buildings were excluded. Where a quite definite and positive visual effect is required from high buildings, the aims would need to be clarified in much more detail.

It should also be remembered that other detailed aspects of the siting of high buildings will normally need to be considered—local focal points, the scale of buildings in a Conservation Area, for example, would need to be taken into consideration alongside the policy aims suggested by views from the surrounding countryside. These other aspects are covered in the townscape survey of specific areas (Maps 9–10). Therefore a final policy aim for high buildings may not be completed until those details are available.

In many towns a more sophisticated survey will be needed, to suggest alternative areas for high buildings. In a very large town a High Buildings Policy may be concerned more with the identities of districts than with the character of the whole town.

Map 6 carries the policy aims for high buildings a stage further. Although certain areas were shown as suitable for high buildings, there would be height restrictions over parts of these areas due to the rise and fall of land. For example, high buildings would be restricted to 75 ft. above ground level in all areas except the bottom of the valley to the east, where they would remain hidden from views from the west and north of the town. High buildings on this site would, however, create a positive new image on approach from the east.

236

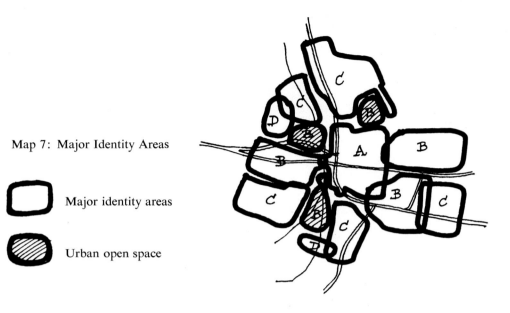

Map 7: Major Identity Areas

▢ Major identity areas

▨ Urban open space

Survey of Townscape

OBJECTIVES: To identify the areas of identity over the whole town, and in detail with specific areas.

To identify the archaeological features and the layout of the town.

To identify the visual qualities of the existing streets in terms of space enclosure and focal points.

To identify the sites of opportunity.

METHOD: Carry out a survey by visual observation and the examination of recorded historic and archaeological evidence of the fabric of the built-up area.

Select the most important local views of focal points.

Mark up the results of observation on a 25 in. or 50 in. to the mile map. The method of annotation of the detailed aspects of townscape is shown on Maps 9–10. The survey should be backed by an illustrated written analysis.

FEATURES TO BE NOTED ON MAP

Major Identity Areas. Map 7 shows the areas of common identity over the town as a whole. It also shows by letter the relationship between the various areas. Area A is the most visually and historically dominant and and Area D the least dominant. This survey covers all areas regardless of architectural quality. It attempts to show areas which hold together as units, because of their overall identity, whether they consist of historic areas, areas of slum property or urban open space.

237

From Map 7 the most dominant major area is clearly the town centre. It is not only the commercial and social centre of the town; it is also the historic core. This area is therefore the most urgent one for detailed consideration.

Local Identity Areas. The local areas will be defined in the same way as the major areas but the survey will pay more attention to architectural detail. Within for example the central area, the new roads will be no more than local distributors or service roads. There may well be a need for a degree of pedestrian segregation over the whole of the town centre area. Map 8 shows the local identity areas.

The local areas are lettered to show the significance of each area, one to the other. Where a group of identity areas is found to exist, the boundaries of a Conservation Area might well coincide with those of the group.

Closely related to the identity areas is the scale of existing development. Map 8 shows the areas which have a greater sense of scale due to the massing of buildings. These places of greater scale usually coincide with the areas with the highest letter for dominance. They suggest where new large-scale development might take place, providing that it does not conflict with conservation aims. Other areas, not so marked, would only be suitable for small-scale development. This aspect is important in formulating high buildings policy and controlling development in the design of infilling.

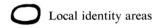 Local identity areas

Areas of greater scale

Map 8: Local Identity Areas

239

Map 9: Townscape—archaeological features

••••▬▬ Line of town walls and existing remains

– – – – Medieval road layout

▬▬▬┐ Original medieval building line

⊔ Ancient river crossing

шшшшшш Earthworks

240

The Townscape in Detail. Maps 9 and 10 cover the detailed visual and architectural qualities of the town centre. The map would normally be accompanied by a written description of certain aspects of the town's history, describing the ancient buildings now demolished and where excavation would be worth while if and when redevelopment takes place, sites on which battles were fought, or other significant local events took place. The major changes in the history of the town, such as the removal of town walls or the abandoning of certain buildings or other features, perhaps a castle or river crossing, would be explained. There would be also an illustrated written statement of other visual qualities. This material would be used in the public statement.

The following features are recorded on the maps.

Map 9

(i) Town walls. The line of the old town walls is shown (this coincides with short lengths of wall which still remain).

(ii) Road layout. The medieval street pattern, still in existence over a considerable part of the town centre, is distinguished by the gridiron layout which contributes to the character of much of the town centre. The bridge now standing on the site of the ancient river crossing is also shown.

Map 10

(iii) Spaces. Spaces which are important to the identity of the town are indicated on the map. The hatched areas imply that the height of buildings around the spaces is important to their enclosure, to the consequent character of the spaces in themselves and the relationship of one space to another.

(iv) Frontages important to street enclosures. Certain frontages, not necessarily with any particular architectural merit, are shown as important to the enclosure of certain additional streets and spaces. This usually includes those which, by being on a curve or a change of direction, close off a view out of the street, There will be no need to mark frontages which are already shown as enclosing a space that is recognised as important to the identity of the town.

(v) Focal points. A number of focal points are shown on the map as well as the principal views towards them. These cover two main types of view; first, local views to focal points within streets and spaces in the area, and second, views across the town where certain buildings are seen from areas outside the town centre—say a residential area or a park. In reverse, certain views are shown from the central area, across the town to the residential areas. These will affect the formulation of a High Buildings Policy.

(vi) Views out to the countryside. The local views out to the countryside from the town centre are shown on the base map. This complements Map 4, which indicates general views from inside the town as a whole.

(vii) Areas of visual opportunity. A number of visual opportunities are shown to exist in the town, for example, the removal of an eyesore or the possibility of replacing a derelict building (A), the better enclosure of a space (B) or where a new building could positively contribute to the street scene in the place of an existing one (C).

242

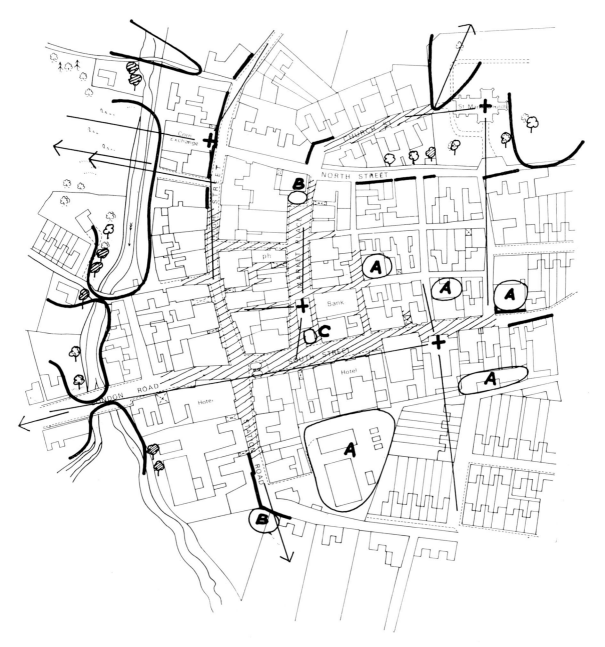

Map 10: Townscape—visual qualities

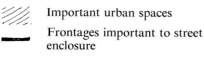
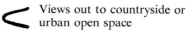
243

Aims for Townscape Discipline. The aims of townscape discipline are to achieve the maximum conservation of all the aspects of the town's character that have been identified. This may mean preserving many of the townscape features such as the road layout, but it will also mean using the discipline of the townscape to influence new development in order to maintain the scale of conservation areas, the adequate enclosure of spaces or, for instance, the dominance of the existing focal points. One of the aims of the townscape discipline will be to suggest the ways in which new development can emphasise the local characteristics of the townscape, perhaps by a pedestrian route following the line of the town wall, or the extension of the gridiron pattern.

The boundaries of major identity areas and those of the local identity areas, indicate possible boundaries for environmental areas. The gaps between the major areas will suggest routes for network roads and the gaps between local identity areas will suggest routes for local distributor or service roads. Where areas overlap, visual or physical links such as pedestrian routes might be maintained. Local identity areas will also suggest visual boundaries to Conservation Areas. See diagrams on pages 51–55 and 131.

The aims of the townscape discipline can be taken to be identical with information recorded in the survey. The interpretation of that information must inevitably be the subject of debate within the planning team, and the effect of the townscape discipline will depend largely upon the influence the architect is able to have within that team.

Survey of Individual Buildings

OBJECTIVES: To identify the buildings of architectural and historic interest and the ancient monuments.

To identify other buildings which can be regarded as permanent and which will continue to affect the visual qualities of the streets in the foreseeable future.

To identify groups of buildings which should be considered as a whole and which include or adjoin historic buildings.

METHOD: Examine the Ministry of Housing's statutory and Supplementary lists of historic buildings and any other local references to other ancient monuments.

Study the groups of buildings by observation in the streets.

Prepare a map showing buildings and groups of buildings to a scale of 25 in. to the mile. This should be supported by an illustrated written description.

245

Map 11: Individual Buildings—Listed
Buildings and groups of buildings

▨▨ Listed buildings (statutory and supplementary)

▢ Other permanent or substantial buildings

▬ Groups of buildings where design discipline for infilling will
operate

FEATURES TO BE NOTED ON A MAP

Listed Buildings, Permanent Buildings and Groups of Buildings. Map 11 shows the buildings of architectural and historical interest in the town centre including all those that it is desirable to preserve but which are not included on existing lists. It also identifies buildings which could be considered as permanent because of their structural condition or value, including, of course, existing new buildings. Groups of buildings are shown in relation to historic buildings where there is a need to maintain cohesion.

The survey of groups of buildings should be backed by photographic elevational records from which drawings can be prepared of each group as a whole. It may be found convenient to prepare scaled drawings from the photographs and the inclusion of a measuring staff in the photographs will simplify the operation. In addition a large-scale plan showing the properties should also be prepared.

This basic material should be supplemented by perspective views taken at intervals down the street to emphasise the shape and enclosure of the street. Views of the street from adjacent areas should also be taken.

Map 12: Conservation Area

― Boundary of conservation area or property boundary

--- Boundary of conservation area across open space

\\\\ Adjoining area of special control

FIRST APPRAISAL OF INDIVIDUAL BUILDINGS

Conservation Areas Policy. The Conservation Areas. Having identified the buildings of architectural and historic interest and the special qualities of townscape, the principal aims of conservation can best be set out by defining a Conservation Area. Map 12 shows the identification of a possible Conservation Area and in addition an adjoining area which would be subject to control because of its proximity to the Conservation Area. The boundaries are drawn to include the historic core of the town where it is intended that change will be only small in scale. It is probable that new major or network roads will be sited away from the central area or in the adjoining areas. A multi-storey car park will be required and this will be placed outside the Conservation Area, to the south. In an area where there is great pressure for change, the boundaries of the Conservation Area would probably be drawn more tightly around the line of the town wall. Where the historic core of the town is extensive, perhaps a mile or two across, a number of Conservation Areas may need to be defined.

Design Discipline for Infilling. The groups with visual cohesion shown on the map will be studied in detail and the group qualities will be analysed in order that any new buildings proposed within them can be seen in relation to the groups as a whole. The aims of the design discipline will be set out in an illustrated statement describing each group of buildings.

The group should first be described as belonging to one of the following three types (see illustrations pages 180–7). (i) the terrace. (ii) The group of similar period but of individual units. (iii) The mixed group of different building periods. This would be followed by a description of the detailed, visual qualities under headings which might include the following: building line, building height and skyline, width of unit, materials, quality of detailing and proportion of window to wall.

The Boundaries of Conservation Areas

On page 52 the designation of conservation areas (under the Civic Amenities Act) was discussed. This section illustrates an approach to drawing the boundaries of these areas: the drawings show some of the factors to be considered, though inevitably there will be minor differences of approach in individual towns. Listed buildings are shown hatched, preferred boundaries in solid lines and less desirable ones in pecked lines. On page 51 it was suggested that the recognition of identity areas could provide the basis on which to establish the extent of a conservation area. This implies that, although also concerned with development control, the designation is basically an aesthetic decision and is not primarily concerned with illuminating the economic problems of conservation.

The fact that an area of architectural or historic quality (or part of such an area) is in no danger or under no particular threat, does not mean it should be omitted. The designation states a general aim, and identifies what is visually or historically important. For example, drawing below, a historic mansion or a church which stands, perhaps in its own grounds, but adjacent to a street regarded as a potential conservation area, would be included in the designated area even though it might not need action to support its preservation. In terms of public relations the qualities of such buildings are obvious to most people and to include them strengthens the perhaps less obvious qualities of the street.

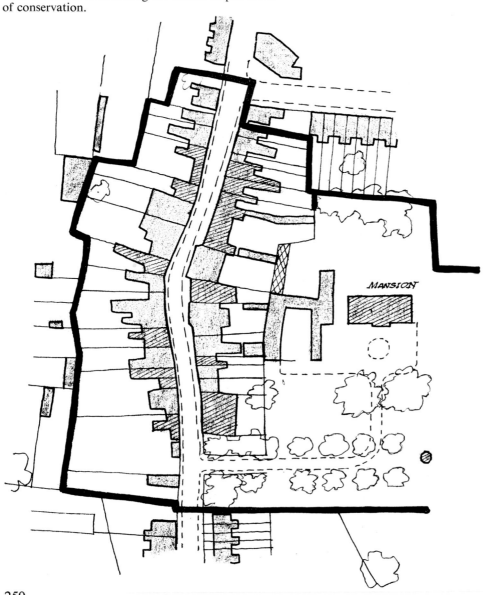

MANSION

250

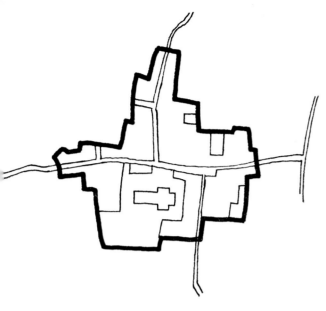

The conservation area should not generally be divided up into complicated parts—a compact central area for example is seldom worth dividing into separate conservation areas. One simple area is usually best and more easily understood at the designation stage.

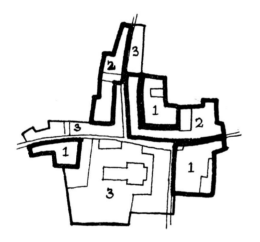

The designation map will need to be backed by a statement of policy, and further maps may be needed to establish areas where different action must take place and where different priorities exist. In the sketch, areas are numbered 1–3 according to priorities for action.

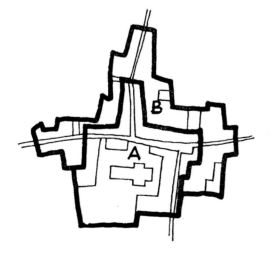

Supplementary policy maps might differentiate between areas of strict preservation (A in sketch), with little new development, and areas where a larger amount of new development would be permitted (B in sketch) but where this development would need to be seen in close visual relationship to the existing townscape within the conservation area.

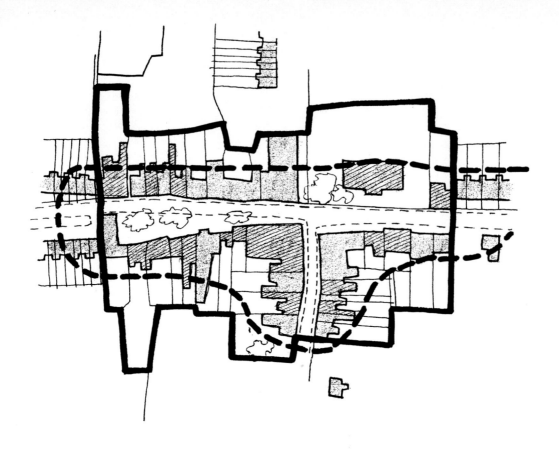

The boundary of the area ought as far as possible
to coincide with property boundaries. Diagrammatic
lines which cut through buildings and sites are
ambiguous and confusing and create difficulties in
development control. Often an area of Special
Advertisement Control or an area over which an
Article IV direction will apply, will need to coincide
with the boundaries of a conservation area and in
these cases a precise line is obviously required to
identify the areas concerned.

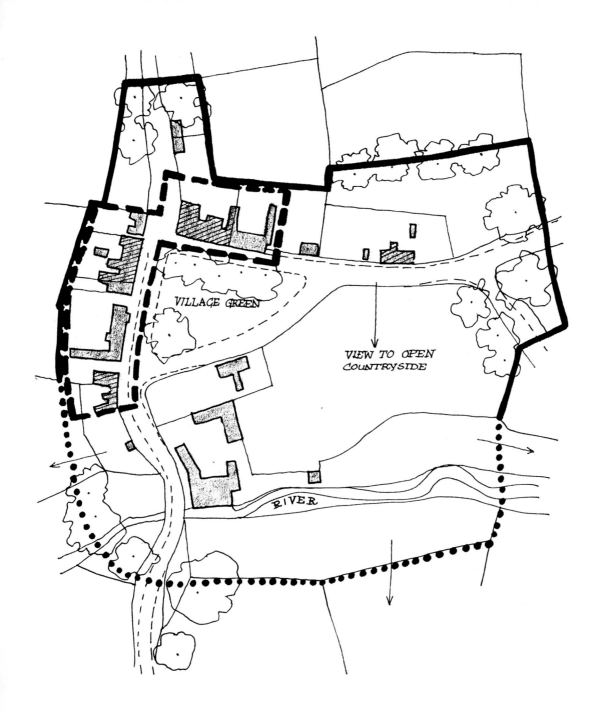

VILLAGE GREEN

VIEW TO OPEN
COUNTRYSIDE

RIVER

In many instances a clear-cut boundary line is difficult to define, particularly where the landscape setting of buildings is concerned. The first consideration ought always to be the retention of complete landscape features, since they are identity areas in themselves. In the plan the whole village green and the surrounding landscape features are retained. Normally, lines of trees and ditches can be used as a boundary line, but where a distant view or the ridge of a hill is important, a dotted line might be used to indicate that no clear boundary exists.

253

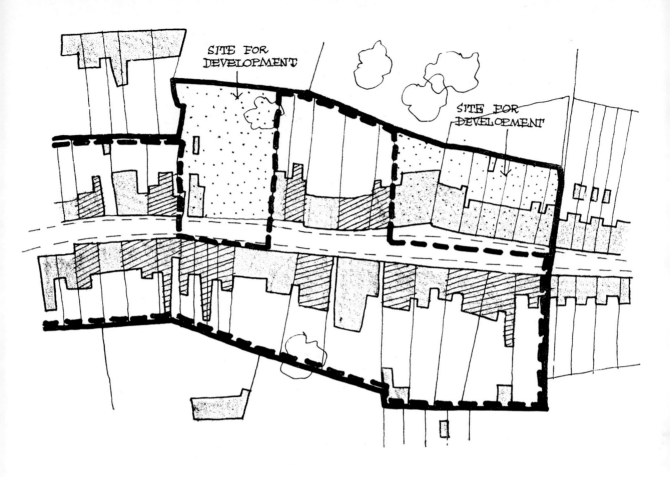

SITE FOR DEVELOPMENT

SITE FOR DEVELOPMENT

The conservation area will often be concerned not only with the preservation of old buildings but also in securing the sympathetic design of new buildings. The boundary should, therefore, include all those sites upon which new development, advertising or landscaping will make a significant impact on the townscape. Again the use of identity areas as the basis of conservation areas will help to determine which sites to include.

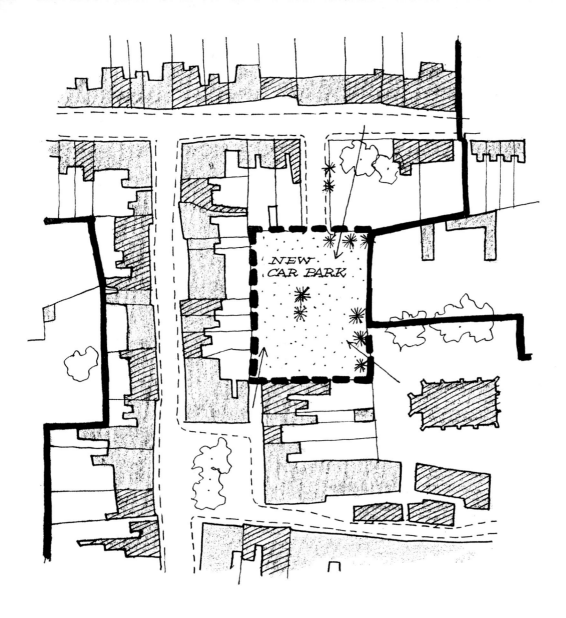

The development of land at the rear of a street,
separate from the buildings to be preserved, can be
controlled because it is in close proximity to the
conservation area. Whether it is necessary to include
such land in the conservation area will depend on the
visual impact of the development and the effect it
will have in land use terms. For example the site of a
car-park might be included if it is to be closely
associated with the buildings in the conservation
area and will be seen as part of the townscape.
Special emphasis might be given to tree-planting in
the car-park as it is in the conservation area.

255

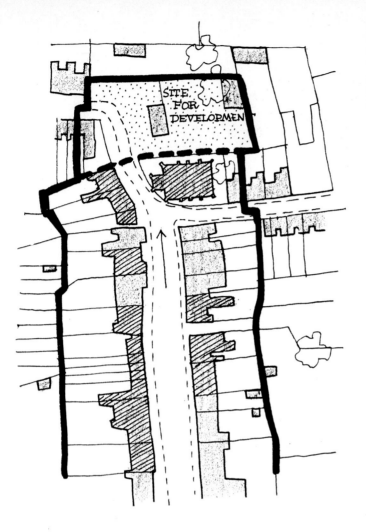

Occasionally it might be felt necessary to include in the area to be designated land which is likely to be re-developed and where new buildings would radically affect the quality of the area. The land at the rear of a focal point in a street might be included for this reason.

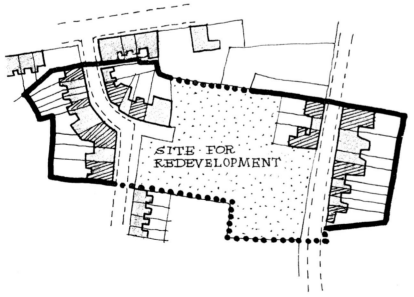

Part of a town might contain two small conservation areas where new development could create the opportunity for a new spatial relationship, bringing the two areas together.

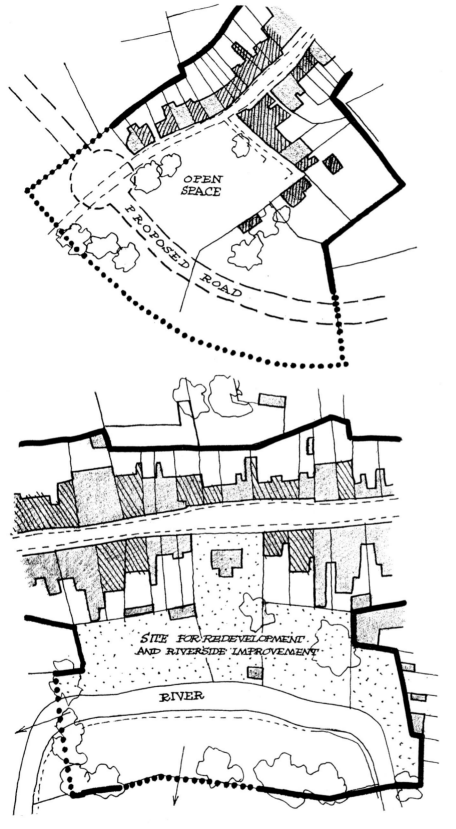

The site for the line of a new road which must inevitably pass through or alongside a conservation area might also be included in the designated area to ensure that the detailing of verges, the design of street lighting and landscaping proposals are seen as part of the conservation area and its character.

OPEN SPACE

PROPOSED ROAD

SITE FOR REDEVELOPMENT AND RIVERSIDE IMPROVEMENT

RIVER

The boundary of the conservation area will usually be drawn to include sites where a positive opportunity exists to improve the townscape as part of the amenity of the area. A riverside improvement scheme might provide an opportunity to improve the quality of a street.

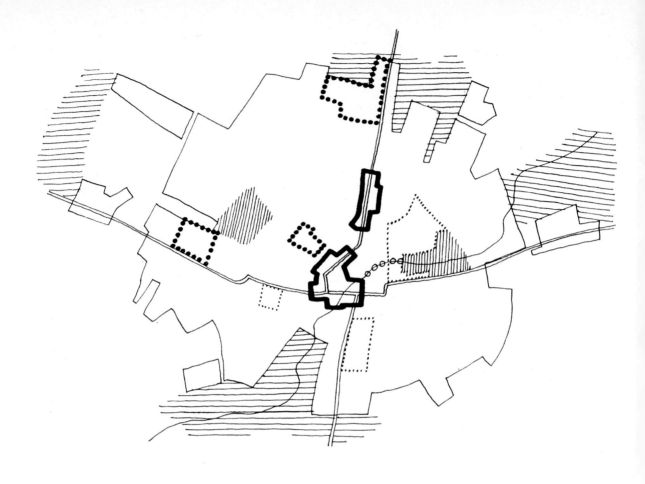

While areas of landscape, which provide the setting for a group of historic buildings, should be included in the designated area, sites of landscape value divorced from areas of architectural or historic value should not in general be designated unless there are archaeological reasons for so doing. Many towns have areas, such as parks and gardens or new housing, which have a high quality of environment and which although of no historic significance nevertheless make a contribution to the character of the town. These may well need some form of identification, but if described as a conservation area, they would probably devalue the special significance of the historic areas. A Town Amenity Map and a written statement showing various areas with different qualities to be protected might be an essential counterpart to the designation of conservation areas and should include the conservation areas on the same map.

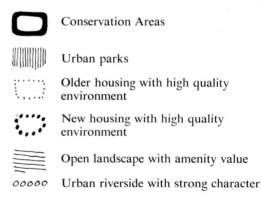

Conservation Areas

Urban parks

Older housing with high quality environment

New housing with high quality environment

Open landscape with amenity value

Urban riverside with strong character

258

BIBLIOGRAPHY

Conservation

THE BUCHANAN REPORT AND HISTORIC TOWNS
  The Council for British Archaeology, Aug 1964.

CONSERVATION AND CONTROL IN BUILT-UP AREAS
  Lord Holford. Paper given at the Town Planning Institute Annual Conference, 1966. Reprinted in the TPI *Journal* June 1966.

CONSERVATION AREAS: PRESERVING THE ARCHITECTURAL AND HISTORIC SCENE
  A survey by the Civic Trust. Civic Trust, 1966, and *Architects' Journal* 18 Jan 1967.

CONSERVATION IN URBAN AREAS
  A report prepared by the County Planning Officers' Society, Mar 1968.

DEVELOPMENT AND THE PRESERVATION OF SITES OF HISTORIC AND ARCHAEOLOGICAL INTEREST
  M. W. Barley. Paper given at Town and Country Planning Summer School, 1956. Report of Proceedings published by the Town Planning Institute.

THE FUTURE OF HISTORIC TOWN CENTRES IN URBAN REPLANNING
  The Earl of Euston. Paper given at the Town Planning Institute Annual Conference, May 1963. TPI *Journal* July/Aug 1963.

HISTORIC TOWNS AND THE PLANNING PROCESS
  Guidance to local authorities. The Council for British Archaeology, Dec 1966.

HISTORIC TOWNS: PRESERVATION AND CHANGE
  Her Majesty's Stationery Office, 1967.

PRESERVATION AFTER BUCHANAN
  Lord Esher. Paper given at the Royal Institute of British Architects Annual Conference, 1964. Reprinted in the RIBA *Journal* June 1964.

PRESERVATION AND CHANGE
  R. R. Worskett. Report of Subject Discussion Group at the Town and Country Planning Summer School, 1966. Published by the Town Planning Institute.

PROGRESS IN CREATING CONSERVATION AREAS
  A series of reports issued by the Civic Trust.

PROTECTION OF AREAS OF ARCHITECTURAL IMPORTANCE
  Report prepared for the Civic Trust Conference on the Civic Amenities Act. Civic Trust 1967.

Preservation Abroad

FRANCE
  New directions in the protection of ancient buildings and groups of buildings, with illustrations of restoration and reconstruction in "Le Secteur Sauvegardé d'Avignon", Robert Brichet. *La Construction Moderne*, No. 1, 1968.

HISTORIC CENTRES
  Special issue of *Urbanistica* on historic centres—research and problems, covering Italy, France, Germany, Poland, Holland, Denmark, Sweden, Czechoslovakia, Jugoslavia and the USA. *Urbanistica* 42–43, Feb 1965. Reprinted as "Historic Urban Areas", in French, German and English, for the International Federation for Housing and Planning. Urbanistica, Turin, 1966.

LISTING AND PRESERVING HISTORIC BUILDINGS
  Anthony Dale.
  1. The European picture. *Architectural Review* Aug 1965.
  2. USA, Canada, S. Africa, Australia and New Zealand. *Architectural Review* Oct 1966.

PRESERVATION AND DEVELOPMENT OF ANCIENT BUILDINGS AND HISTORICAL OR ARTISTIC SITES
  Council of Europe, Strasbourg, France, 1963.

PRESERVING HISTORIC AMERICA
  United States Department of Housing and Urban Development, Washington, June 1966.

SITES HISTORIQUES URBAINS
  Special issue covering preservation of historic towns in Germany, Czechoslovakia, France and Switzerland. *Urbanisme*, Number 101, France, 1967.

Trees and Landscape

LANDSCAPE: A CONTEMPORARY COMMENT
G. P. Youngman. RIBA *Journal* June 1965.
MOVING BIG TREES
Civic Trust, 1966.
TOMORROW'S LANDSCAPE
Sylvia Crowe. Architectural Press, 1956.
TREES FOR TOWN AND COUNTRY
Brenda Colvin. Lund Humphries, 1961.
TREES: INCLUDING PRESERVATION, PLANTING, LAW AND HIGHWAYS
Ronald J. Morling. Estates Gazette Limited. 1st edition 1954. Revised 1963.
TREES IN TOWN AND CITY
Her Majesty's Stationery Office, 1958.

High Buildings

HIGH BUILDINGS IN OXFORD
Oxford City Architect and Planning Office, 1962.
LIVERPOOL: HIGH BUILDINGS POLICY
Liverpool City Planning Department, 1965.
THE SITING OF HIGH BUILDINGS
Alec Clifton-Taylor. *Country Life*, 14 Oct, 1965
UP AND OUT
J. R. Nichols. *Architectural Review* Dec 1964.

Townscape

ARCHITECTURE—CITY SENSE
Theo Crosby. Studio Vista, 1965.
BRITISH TOWNSCAPE
Ewart Johns. Edward Arnold, 1965.
CITIES
Special issue of *Scientific American*, edited by Dennis Flanagan *et al*. Sept 1965. Reprinted as "CITIES: A Scientific American Book", Penguin Books, 1967.
CITY PLANNING, ACCORDING TO ARTISTIC PRINCIPLES
Camillo Sitte, translated by George and Christiane Collins. Columbia University Studies in Art History and Archaeology. Phaidon, 1965.
COUNTER ATTACK
Ian Nairn. Architectural Press, 1957.
DESIGN AND DETAIL OF SPACE BETWEEN BUILDINGS
Elisabeth Beazley. Architectural Press, 1963.
DESIGN IN TOWN AND VILLAGE
(Including sections by Thomas Sharp, Sir Frederick Gibberd and Lord Holford.) Her Majesty's Stationery Office, 1953.
DESIGN OF CITIES
Edmund N. Bacon. Thames and Hudson, 1967.
ENGLISH PANORAMA
Thomas Sharp. Architectural Press, 1950 (1st edition 1936).
HOUSING AND DEVELOPMENT
R. C. Stones. *Town Planning Review* Jan 1967.
THE IMAGE OF THE CITY
Kevin Lynch. Joint Center for Urban Studies of the Massachusetts Institute of Technology and Harvard University, M.I.T. Press and Harvard University Press, 1964 (reprint).
ITALIAN TOWNSCAPE
Ivor de Wolfe. Architectural Press, 1963.
LANDSCAPE IN DISTRESS
Lionel Brett. Architectural Press, 1965.
LETTERING ON BUILDINGS
Nicolete Gray. Architectural Press, 1960.

260

LIVING IN TOWNS
  Maurice Barley and Patrick Nuttgens. BBC Publication, 1966.
OUTRAGE
  Ian Nairn. Architectural Press, 1955.
REGENT'S CANAL: A POLICY FOR ITS FUTURE
  Regent's Canal Group, 10 Vincent Terrace, London N.1. 1967.
THE SHAPE OF TOWNS
  (Looking and Seeing, Number 4.) Kurt Rowland. Ginn and Co., 1966.
SIGNS IN ACTION
  James Sutton. Studio Vista, 1965.
SOME REFLECTIONS ON THE GEOGRAPHICAL DESCRIPTION AND ANALYSIS OF TOWNSCAPE
  A. E. Smailes. Institute of British Geographers. *Transactions and Papers* 1955.
THE TOWN
  G. Martin. Vista Books, 1961.
TOWN DESIGN
  Frederick Gibberd. Architectural Press, 5th edition, 1967.
TOWNS AND BUILDINGS
  Steen Eiler Rasmussen. Liverpool University Press, 1951.
TOWNSCAPE
  Gordon Cullen. Architectural Press, 1961.
TYNE LANDSCAPE
  A survey of the river corridor with proposals for landscape renewal. I. C. Laurie. 1965. (Available from Newcastle City Planning Office.)
URBAN AESTHETICS
  Tony Meats. *Architecture East Midlands* Feb/Mar 1967.
URBAN STRUCTURING
  Studies of Alison and Peter Smithson. Studio Vista, 1967.
THE VILLAGE: PHYSICAL STRUCTURE
  Official Architecture and Planning June 1966.
VILLAGE PLANNING: THE VITAL THIRD DIMENSION
  Anthony Goss. *Official Architecture and Planning* Sept 1964.

Infilling

CIVIC TRUST AWARDS
  Reports of Annual Awards for 1965, 1966 and 1967, Civic Trust.
NEW BUILDINGS FOR OLD TOWNS
  Sir Hugh Casson. *Proceedings* of Georgian Group Conference, 1953.
NEW BUILDINGS IN OLD TOWNS
  Alec Clifton-Taylor. *Country Life* 21st July, 1966 and 28 July, 1966.

Architectural History

ARCHITECTURE OF ENGLAND FROM PREHISTORIC TIMES TO THE PRESENT DAY
  Doreen Yarwood. Batsford, 1963.
ARCHITECTURE IN BRITAIN 1530–1830
  Sir John Summerson. Pelican History of Art. Penguin Books, 4th edition, 1963.
ARCHITECTURE: NINETEENTH AND TWENTIETH CENTURIES
  H. R. Hitchcock. Pelican History of Art. Penguin Books, 1955.
BUILDINGS OF ENGLAND
  Series (by counties) written and edited by Nikolaus Pevsner. Penguin Books.

Restoration and Repair of Buildings

THE CARE OF OLD BUILDINGS
  A Practical Guide for Architects and Owners. Donald W. Insall. Reprinted by *The Architects Journal* for the Society for the Protection of Ancient Buildings, 1958.
THE CONVERSION OF OLD BUILDINGS INTO NEW HOMES, FOR OCCUPATION AND INVESTMENT
  C. Bernard Brown. Batsford, 1955.
A GUIDE TO HISTORIC BUILDINGS LAW
  Cambridgeshire and Isle of Ely County Planning Department, Sept 1967

HISTORIC BUILDINGS: PROBLEMS OF THEIR PRESERVATION
  June Hargreaves. York Civic Trust, May 1964.
HOUSE CONVERSION AND IMPROVEMENT
  Felix Walter. Architectural Press, 1956.
NEW USES FOR OLD CHURCHES
  Report of the York Redundant Churches Commission. (Available from the Church Information Office and SPCK.) 1967.
THE PATTERN OF ENGLISH BUILDING
  Alec Clifton-Taylor. Batsford, 1962.

General Planning

BRITISH TOWNS: A STATISTICAL STUDY OF THEIR SOCIAL AND ECONOMIC DIFFERENCES
  C. A. Moser and Wolf Scott. Centre for Urban Studies *Report* No. 2. Oliver and Boyd, 1961.
CITIZENS' GUIDE TO TOWN AND COUNTRY PLANNING
  D. W. Riley, for the Town and Country Planning Association, 1966.
THE CITY IN HISTORY
  Lewis Mumford. Secker and Warburg, 1961; and Pelican, 1961.
A CITY IS NOT A TREE
  Christopher Alexander. *Architectural Forum* April and May 1965; *Design* Feb 1966.
CONTROL OF OUTDOOR ADVERTISING
  Comments from planning authorities on the effectiveness of advertisement control. *Town and Country Planning* Feb 1962.
DEATH AND LIFE OF GREAT AMERICAN CITIES
  Jane Jacobs. Random House, New York, 1961; Jonathan Cape, London 1962; Penguin, 1964.
FOOT STREETS IN FOUR CITIES
  (Dusseldorf, Essen, Cologne, Copenhagen.) Report Number 3, Norwich City Planning Office, Nov 1966.
THE FUTURE OF DEVELOPMENT PLANS
  Report of the Planning Advisory Group. Her Majesty's Stationery Office, 1965.
THE GEOGRAPHY OF TOWNS
  Arthur Smailes. Hutchinson University Library, 1953. 5th edition (paperback), 1966.
HOW TO FIND OUT IN ARCHITECTURE AND BUILDING
  A guide to sources of information. D. L. Smith. Pergamon Press, 1967.
THE LAND OF BRITAIN: ITS USE AND MISUSE
  Professor Dudley Stamp. Longmans, 1962.
PLANNING CONTROL OF SIGNS AND POSTERS
  Her Majesty's Stationery Office, 1966.
TOWNS AND CITIES
  Emrys Jones. (Opus 13, Oxford Paperbacks University Series.) Oxford University Press, 1966.
URBAN FORM IN THE REGIONAL CONTEXT
  Shean McConnell. *Official Architecture and Planning* Jan 1967.

Traffic

MIXED BLESSING—THE MOTOR IN BRITAIN
  C. D. Buchanan. Leonard Hill, 1958.
MORE TRAFFIC IN TOWNS
  C. D. Buchanan. Paper given at the Royal Institute of British Architects Annual Conference, 1966. RIBA *Journal* Oct 1966.
PLANNING FOR MAN AND MOTOR
  Paul Ritter. Pergamon Press, 1964.
REDEVELOPMENT OF CENTRAL AREAS IN THE LIGHT OF THE BUCHANAN REPORT
  A. M. MacEwen. *Town Planning Institute Journal* Jan 1965.
TRAFFIC IN TOWNS
  A study of the long-term problems of traffic in urban areas (The Buchanan Report). Her Majesty's Stationery Office, 1963; Penguin Books, 1963 (shortened version).
THE VIEW FROM THE ROAD
  Donald Appleyard, Kevin Lynch and John R. Myer. Joint Center for Urban Studies of the Massachusetts Institute of Technology and Harvard University. MIT Press, Cambridge, Massachusetts, 1964.

Shopping

CHANGING SHOPPING HABITS AND THEIR IMPACT ON TOWN PLANNING
W. L. Waide. Paper given at the Town Planning Institute Annual Conference, 1963; reprinted TPI *Journal* Sept/Oct 1963.

PEDESTRIANISED SHOPPING STREETS IN EUROPE
A comparative study. John G. Gray. Pedestrians' Association for Road Safety, Edinburgh and District Branch, 1965.

SHOPPING CENTRES IN BRITAIN
R. N. Percival. TPI *Journal* Sept/Oct 1965.

SHOPPING CENTRES: TRAFFIC AND ECONOMIC ASPECTS
Cost/benefit approach as basis for assessing claims of redevelopment schemes. H. D. Peake. *Surveyor and Municipal Engineer* 28 Jan 1967.

SUPERMARKETS
Elisabeth Beazley. *Architectural Review* Nov 1966.

WHY HALLMARK GOT OUT OF TOWN
Too many shops. The end of the property boom. Oliver Marriott, *The Times* 12 May 1967.

Town Studies

AR = *Architectural Review.*

HISTORIC TOWNS
List of towns with historic centres meriting preservation. Council for British Archaeology. July, 1965.

BATH: A PLANNING AND TRANSPORT STUDY
Colin Buchanan & Partners, 1965. Supplementary Report, 1966.

BATH, A STUDY IN CONSERVATION
Colin Buchanan & Partners. Her Majesty's Stationery Office, 1968.

BATH
Townscape. William Carr and John Kelsey. AR Oct 1964.

BECCLES: SURVEY AND APPRAISAL 1966
East Suffolk County Planning Department, 1966.

BECCLES: TOWN MAP 1967
(Draft Town Map Review 1967 and Draft Town Centre Map.) East Suffolk County Planning Department, 1967.

BEVERLEY'S LIFELINE
Townscape. Ian Nairn. AR Feb 1963.

BEVERLEY
Perspective—East Yorkshire (Journal of the Yorks and East Yorks Arch Soc.) Mar/Apr 1967.

BEWDLEY
Midland Experiment—A study in townscape prepared by the Extra-Mural Department of the University of Birmingham and the *Architectural Review.* AR Nov 1953.

BISHOP'S STORTFORD
The obscure logic of redevelopment. James Stovel. *Official Architecture and Planning* June 1966.

BRADFORD-ON-AVON
Townscape. Richard Reid. AR Oct 1965.

BRIDGNORTH, SHROPSHIRE
Structure of small towns. Basil Honikman. *Official Architecture and Planning* Dec 1966.

BRIGHTON
Fashionable Brighton 1820–1860. Anthony Dale. Oriel Press, second edition, 1967.

BRIGHTON SQUARE
A town-planning triumph. *Concrete Quarterly*, Oct/Dec 1967.

BRISTOL AND ITS ARCHITECTS
Diana Rowntree. RIBA *Journal* Feb 1966.

CAMBRIDGE: DREAMING SPIRES AND TEEMING TOWERS
The character of Cambridge. Thomas Sharp. Liverpool University Press, 1963 (reprinted from the *Town Planning Review*, Jan 1963).

CANTERBURY: HISTORIC TOWN OR WRITE-OFF?
Townscape. Lewis Braithwaite. AR. Oct 1967.

CHESTER, A STUDY IN CONSERVATION
Donald W. Insall & Partners. Her Majesty's Stationery Office, 1968.

CHESTER: THE CHALLENGE OF CHANGE
Sidney H. Tasker. *Town Planning Review* Oct 1966. (Reprinted in *Architecture North West*, Feb 1968.)
CHICHESTER, A STUDY IN CONSERVATION
G. S. Burrows. County Planning Officer, West Sussex. Her Majesty's Stationery Office, 1968.
CHICHESTER: PRESERVATION AND PROGRESS
Report by the County Planning Office, West Sussex County Council, 1966.
CHICHESTER
Cathedral cities. Townscape. Ian Nairn and Kenneth Browne. AR Sept 1963.
COLCHESTER: AN HISTORIC TOWNSCAPE
Essex County Council and Colchester Borough Council, 1967
DENSHAW
The missing hill towns. Townscape. Ian Nairn. AR Sept 1964.
DIGGLE
The missing hill towns. Townscape. Ian Nairn. AR Sept 1964.
DISS
Townscape. Kenneth Browne. AR Feb 1966.
DURHAM ENDANGERED
Andor Gomme. AR June 1960.
DURSLEY
Townscape. University of Bristol and Gordon Cullen. AR July 1956.
EDENBRIDGE: THE LAST CHANCE
Townscape. Kenneth Browne. AR Nov 1965.
EDGWORTH
The missing hill towns. Townscape. Ian Nairn. AR Sept 1964.
ETON
A Future for Eton. Buckinghamshire Departments of Architecture and Planning. Jan 1968.
EVESHAM
Midland experiment. A study in townscape prepared by the Extra-Mural Department of the University of Birmingham and the *Architectural Review* AR Feb 1954.
EXETER: OLD AND NEW TOWNSCAPE
Ewart Johns. *Town and Country Planning* July 1964.
FARNHAM: DEAD OR ALIVE?
Townscape. Ian Nairn and Kenneth Browne. AR Aug 1961.
FAVERSHAM, KENT
Christopher Hussey. *Country Life* 6 Jan, 13 Jan, 3 Feb 1966.
GLASGOW: PARK CIRCUS AREA
Corporation of Glasgow Planning Department, 1967.
GLASGOW: "THE SECOND CITY"
C. A. Oakley. Blackie, 1967.
GLOUCESTER: THE VIEW OF THE CATHEDRAL
Extracts from G. A. Jellicoe's "A Height of Buildings Policy" for Gloucester. AR July 1966.
GLOUCESTER
Cathedral cities. Townscape. Ian Nairn and Kenneth Browne. AR Sept 1963.
GRANTHAM
Kenneth Fennell. *Architecture East Midlands* 15 June 1965.
HASTINGS: THE OLD TOWN
Report on its conservation and development by Lord Holford and R. A. Haskell. Hastings Town Planning Office, 1966.
HEREFORD
Cathedral cities. Townscape. Ian Nairn and Kenneth Browne. AR Sept 1963.
IRONBRIDGE
Kenneth Brown and Ian Nairn. Townscape. AR June 1963.
KING'S LYNN: THE HISTORIC CORE
A study and plan. E. V. Chesterton, in association with Leonard Manesseh and Partners, 1964.
LANCASHIRE MILL TOWNS
Townscape. Studies of Preston, Bolton, Blackburn, Bury, Burnley and Rochdale. Ian Nairn. AR July 1962.
LAVENHAM: PAST, PRESENT, FUTURE
Donald Insall. West Suffolk County Council, 1961.
LLANTRISANT: A WELSH HILL TOWN
An Environmental Study. Gordon Cullen. Glamorgan County Planning Office, 1968.

264

LINCOLN, STEEP HILL
Ian Nairn. Townscape. AR Sept 1961.
LIVERPOOL: SEAPORT, ARCHITECTURE AND TOWNSCAPE IN LIVERPOOL
Quentin Hughes. Lund Humphries, 1965.
A LIVERPOOL NOTEBOOK
Gordon Cullen. AR April 1965.
LUDLOW
Midland experiment. A study in townscape prepared by the Extra-Mural Department of the University of Birmingham and the *Architectural Review*. AR Sept 1953.
MALDON: SEVERED OR SERVED
Townscape. Kenneth Browne. AR Aug 1966.
MOUSELOW
The missing hill towns. Townscape. Ian Nairn. AR Sept 1964.
NEWCASTLE: CITY OLD AND NEW
Northern Architect July 1966.
NEWCASTLE-UPON-TYNE: HISTORIC ARCHITECTURE OF NEWCASTLE
Edited by Bruce Allsopp. Oriel Press, 1967.
NEWARK RENEWED
Introduction by H. J. Lowe. *Architecture East Midlands* Feb–Mar 1966.
NORWICH: REVITALISATION APPRAISAL
City of Norwich Planning Department, 1966.
OXFORD OBSERVED
Thomas Sharp. County Life Limited, 1952.
OXFORD REPLANNED
Thomas Sharp. Published for the Oxford City Council by the Architectural Press, 1948.
PETERSFIELD, HAMPSHIRE
Official Architecture and Planning Nov 1966.
PLYMOUTH BARBICAN
Townscape. Gordon Cullen. AR April 1957.
POOLE, DORSET: NEW HOPE FOR THE OLD TOWN
L. Myers. *Architects' Journal* 4 Aug 1965.
SALISBURY
Cathedral cities. Townscape. Ian Nairn and Kenneth Browne. AR Sept 1963.
SALISBURY: TOWN CENTRE PLAN
Wiltshire County Council, 1965.
SEVENOAKS: SEVERED OR LINKED?
Richard Reid and William Carr. Townscape. AR May 1965.
SHEPTON MALLET
Gordon Cullen. AR Sept 1957.
SHREWSBURY
Midland experiment. A study in townscape prepared by the Extra-Mural Department of the University of Birmingham and the *Architectural Review*. AR May 1954.
STAMFORD: TOWN CENTRE HISTORIC AREAS POLICY
County of Lincoln. Parts of Kesteven. 1st report 1963; 2nd report 1966.
STONE: ITS FUTURE APPEARANCE
Guidance for the control of the built environment. Graham W. Ashworth. *Town Planning Review*, Jan 1968.
TENTERDEN EXPLORED
An Architectural and Townscape Analysis. Frederick Macmanus & Partners and Gordon Cullen. Kent County Council, 1967.
TENTERDEN: A PLAN FOR THE TOWN CENTRE
Kent County Planning Department, 1967.
TEWKESBURY: AN ARCHITECTURAL AND HISTORICAL BUILDING SURVEY
Gloucestershire County Council, 1966.
THAXTED: A SOCIAL AND ECONOMIC SURVEY
Essex County Planning Department, 1965.
THAXTED: AN HISTORICAL AND ARCHITECTURAL SURVEY
Donald Insall and Associates. Essex County Council, 1967.
TONBRIDGE: OPPORTUNITY LOST OR FOUND?
Townscape. J. R. Nichols. AR May 1964.

TROWBRIDGE
Townscape. Gordon Cullen. AR Feb 1958.
TUNBRIDGE WELLS: A WALK IN SPACE—A STUDY OF THE PANTILES
Kenneth Browne. AR Dec 1965.
WINCHESTER
Cathedral cities. Townscape. Ian Nairn and Kenneth Browne. AR Sept 1963.
WITNEY
Conservation Study, Number 1. Oxfordshire County Architect's Department, Sept 1967.
WORCESTER
Cathedral cities. Townscape. Ian Nairn and Kenneth Browne. AR Sept 1963.
YORK, A STUDY IN CONSERVATION
Brett & Pollen. Her Majesty's Stationery Office, 1968.
YORK: REPORT ON PROPOSED CONSERVATION AREAS
York City Engineer and Planning Officer, March 1968.
YORK AND ITS ARCHITECTS
Diana Rowntree. RIBA *Journal* June 1965.

Town Studies: London

WEST KENTISH TOWN
Town Planning Consultant's Report No. 3, 1964.
Armstrong & Macmanus, with Cullen, Browne and Nairn for the former St. Pancras Borough Council.
A LATIN QUARTER FOR LONDON: A TOWNSCAPE SURVEY OF COVENT GARDEN AND A PLAN FOR ITS FUTURE
Kenneth Browne. AR Mar 1964.
WEST END: A SERIES OF TOWNSCAPE ARTICLES
Kenneth Browne. *Architectural Review.*
1. Trafalgar Square   June 1966
2. Soho   July 1966
3. South Bank   Oct 1966
4. Theatreland   Dec 1966
5. Mayfair   Feb 1967
6. Whitehall area   May 1967
7. Pimlico   Sept 1967
8. Bloomsbury   Dec 1967
BRENTFORD RIVERSIDE
A townscape study of the effect of recent planning proposals on its scale and character. Kenneth Browne. AR Sept 1965.

ORGANISATIONS concerned with Preservation and the Environment

Official Organisations

COUNCIL OF INDUSTRIAL DESIGN   28 Haymarket, London sw1. 01 839 8000.
Concerned with the improvement of the design of industrial products, including street furniture. Maintains the Design Index of products, the Design Centre and other changing exhibitions.

HISTORIC BUILDINGS COUNCIL
England: Sanctuary Buildings, Great Smith Street, London sw1. 01 222 7790.
Responsible to the Ministry of Housing and Local Government.
Scotland: 21 Hill Street, Edinburgh 2. 031 226 5208.
Responsible to the Scottish Home and Health Department.
Wales: Summit House, Windsor Place, Cardiff. 0222. 42331.
Responsible to the Welsh Office.
Gives grants to buildings of outstanding architectural or historic value, and will give advice to the public.

NATIONAL BUILDINGS RECORD
England: Fielden House, 10 Great College Street, London sw1. 01 930 6554.
Scotland: 52–54 Melville Street, Edinburgh 3. 031 225 5994/5.
Set up under the Royal Commission for Historic Monuments.
Keeps records and photographs of historic buildings.

ROYAL FINE ART COMMISSION
England: 2 Carlton Gardens, London sw1. 01 930 3935.
Scotland: 22 Melville Street, Edinburgh 3. 031 225 5434.
Enquires into and advises upon questions of public amenity and artistic importance.

Non-Official Organisations

ANCIENT MONUMENTS SOCIETY   12 Edwardes Square, London w8. 01 937 1414.
Concerned with the conservation of places of historic interest, ancient monuments, historic buildings, etc. Makes representations to those concerned with ancient monuments to ensure their maintenance, and gives small grants.

CIVIC TRUST   18 Carlton House Terrace, London sw1. 01 930 0914.
Aims to promote high standards of architecture and planning, and rouse public interest through local amenity societies, with the help of exhibitions, conferences, films and publications.

COUNCIL FOR BRITISH ARCHAEOLOGY   8 St. Andrew's Place, London nw1. 01 486 1527.
Advises societies and individuals on items of archaeological interest.

COUNCIL FOR THE PRESERVATION OF RURAL ENGLAND   4 Hobart Place, London sw1. 01 235 4771.
Provides advice and information to the public to secure the protection of the countryside, country towns and villages.

COUNCIL FOR THE PROTECTION OF RURAL WALES   Pen-y-lan, Meifod, Montgomeryshire. Meifod 383.
As the CPRE.

GEORGIAN GROUP   2 Chester Street, London sw1. 01 235 3081.
Aims to arouse public interest in Georgian architecture and town planning, and advises on the preservation of buildings, streets and squares of merit.

NATIONAL TRUST
England: 42 Queen Anne's Gate, London sw1. 01 930 0211.
Scotland: 5 Charlotte Square, Edinburgh 2. 031 225 2184.
Preserves lands and buildings of beauty or historic interest for the benefit of the nation. Owns over 200 historic buildings and about 400,000 acres of land in England, Wales and Northern Ireland.

PILGRIM TRUST   Millbank House, 2 Great Peter Street, London sw1. 01 222 4231.
Makes grants for the repair of ancient buildings and works of art.

SOCIETY FOR THE PROTECTION OF ANCIENT BUILDINGS   55 Great Ormond Street, London wc1. 01 405 2646.
Concerned with the protection of buildings of architectural beauty and historic interest, especially those built before 1714. Advises on restoration of buildings and planning problems, and keeps a list of threatened houses for possible purchase.

TOWN AND COUNTRY PLANNING ASSOCIATION   The Planning Centre, 28 King Street, Covent Garden, London wc2. 01 836 5006/7.

Founded to promote a national policy of land-use planning, the improvement of living and working conditions, the maintenance of the green belt, good farm land and national amenities, with particular emphasis on new and expanded towns. Arranges meetings and discussion groups, publishes a monthly journal and the weekly Planning Bulletin.

VICTORIAN SOCIETY   12, Magnolia Wharf, Strand-on-the-Green, London w4. 01 994 1510.

Promotes interest in Victorian and Edwardian buildings and aims to ensure their preservation. Arranges walks, lectures, etc.

ACKNOWLEDGEMENTS

Aerofilms: 184 top. Architect and Building News: 210 bottom (photo Colin Westwood). Civic Trust: 180 centre and bottom (architect Ernest F. Tew, photo R. F. Wills); 182 bottom left (architect Henry Faulkner Brown, photo D. Gordon Swinton); 182 bottom right (architects C. H. Elsom & Partners, photo R. F. Wills); 185 top (architects Sir Hugh Casson, Neville Conder & Partners, photo Henk Snoek); 199 top (architect Frederick McManus & Partners, photo John McCann). Enfield Civic Society: 120. National Monuments Record 21 top and bottom, 24 top right, 45 top, 129 both. Andrew Renton and Associates (architects) 204 (photo Henk Snoek). Sir Frederick Gibberd and Partners (photo Henk Snoek) 142 top left. York Corporation 211 both. Ordnance maps are reproduced from the Ordnance Survey map with the sanction of the Controller of H.M. Stationery Office: Crown copyright reserved.

INDEX of Places

INDEX of Architects